MOTHERHOOD AND HOLLYWOOD

Villard / New York

PATRICIA HEATON

MOTHER HOOD

and HOLLY WOOD

HOW TO GET A JOB LIKE MINE

Library of Congress Cataloging-in-Publication Data
Heaton, Patricia.
Motherhood and Hollywood / Patricia Heaton.
p.   cm.
ISBN 0-375-50871-6
1. Heaton, Patricia.   2. Actors—United States—Biography.   I. Title.
PN2287.H393 A3 2002
791.45'028'092—dc21   2002071399
[B]

Villard Books website address: www.villard.com

Printed in the United States of America on acid-free paper

24689753

First Edition

Book design by Casey Hampton

TO MY MOM

with deep gratitude for my life

ACKNOWLEDGMENTS

This whole thing started with Dr. Bob, so right away I want to thank Robert Hamilton, our pediatrician and dear friend. He suggested I write a book after he roped me into giving a speech at a pediatrician's dinner at UCLA. So thank you, Bob. For that and a lot more. My terrific agents at UTA, Martin Lesak and Howie Sanders, ran with the idea, and Howie hooked me up with the elegant, eloquent, and very savvy Mort Janklow, who held my hand and skillfully steered me through the world of publishing, all while vacationing in Europe. I thank Bruce Tracy for his thoughtfulness regarding the book and his humor and friendship, and all my new friends at Villard, especially the copy editor, Randee Marullo. My lawyer, Bill Skrzyniarz, not only takes complete care of everything and is a good friend to boot, but also has more consonants than vowels in his last name, which intimidates people. I like that. And Dana Fineman-Appel, my cover photographer, went out of her way to help me in a tight spot, with glorious results.

Acknowledgments

Throughout the book, I've mentioned many whom I've had the great good fortune to know so far in my life; there are a few more that deserve recognition. Barbara Tepper, Martha Mattingly, and RoseMarie Taglione (and her husband, Anthony) were my dear coworkers in New York, and I keep in touch with them to this day. Eric Scott Kincaid, Kirsten Lind, and Meryl Goodfader are all friends from the trenches of the acting world still fighting the good fight. I still have good friends from my experience with Stage Three in New York, including James Ryan and Jordan Roberts (and Marianne), and I hope all the rest of the company are happy and well. The irrepressible Donna Parish was my roommate in New York and became a dear friend, all because I answered an ad in *The Village Voice*. You never know.

And Ohio State wouldn't have been the same (or as insane) without Susie, Sally, Kristy, Robyn, Mindy, Kelly, Monica, Camille, and Rick. They put up with my laziness, craziness, and sloppiness, and came to see me in *The Bald Soprano*, a real test of anyone's friendship.

Almost every friendship I made in Los Angeles started from a church group or a theater group, so thanks to the Santa Monica Vineyard's Mother's Group, for all their prayers and casseroles; Gail and Jay Caress, for sharing their love and family with me; and Coleman and Caryl Luck, who strong-armed Dave into marrying me and then let us have our reception in their backyard. And I much appreciated the kindness of all from the actors' group who served drinks and manned the bar at my wedding.

David and Brenda Hayward and Steve Itkin helped me sur-

vive my first Los Angeles theater experience with Quincy
Long's wonderful play *The Johnstown Vindicator,* and I thank
the cast, crew, and the theater owners, wherever they all are.
Ditto with my second play, *The Secret Sits in the Middle*; it gave
me the privilege to work with and love Amy Glazer and Marcy
Ross.

My spiritual life would be next to zero if I didn't have the
support and prayers of my girlfriends Lucinda Jenney, Mary
O'Neil, Sarah Rush, Donna Bullock, and Marie Bescancon.
And when I need to hear it from a professional, I have always
been able to count on Dr. Dale and Kathy Brunner, Dr. Dallas
and Jane Willard, and especially, Dr. Timothy and Kathy
Keller, whose classes and tapes have been invaluable.

I don't know exactly how to fit this in smoothly, but I must
thank my decorator Bebe Johnson and her husband, Scott
Carter, for their friendship, or I'll never get my sconces.

Carla Iacampo made sure all my babies got here safely, and
Mark Hyman makes sure *I'm* okay after having them.

My assistant, Julie, and my nanny, Malin, are the only reason my kids and I are dressed, fed, and occasionally on time for
things.

I wouldn't have the career I have today if it weren't for the
following people: William Esper, the most ruthless and, thus,
kindest acting teacher ever; anyone who ever rejected me for a
job, and, more important, those who hired me, especially Ed
Zwick and Marshall Herskovitz, who gave me my first good job
in Los Angeles; Linda Lavin, my mentor and friend; and, especially, Phil and Monica Rosenthal, Ray Romano, Peter Boyle,
Brad Garrett, and Doris Roberts, and all the writers and crew of

Everybody Loves Raymond, with whom I've had the good fortune to share the past six years of my life.

As always, there is the love, support, and prayers of my dad, Chuck, and stepmom, Cece, along with Sharon, Alice, and Franny.

This book would not have been written without the help of my brother, Michael Heaton, who started out as one of my worst childhood enemies and has ended up becoming one of my closest friends.

Last but not least, I thank God every day for my sons, Sam, John, Joe, and Dan, and most of all for my husband, David Hunt, who is in it for the long haul.

CONTENTS

Contents

INTRODUCTION

THIS IS MY FIRST BOOK.

Not to worry. I have *extensive* writing experience. I write all the time. In fact, I've been writing all the time for a long time. (I feel like I'm using the word *time* too much.)

I kept a diary for about two months in 1970. It is the source of a lot of material in this book. However, I've eliminated references to "my monthly friend," my suggestion that we kids buy Dad a leisure suit for his birthday, and mention of any crush I may or may not have had on Davy Jones.

In the fourth grade I wrote a report on blue whales.

I've written letters home from camp ("Please come get me *now*"), written embarrassing poems after reading "The Prophet" by Kahlil Gibran. I've written notes to the school explaining that my kids are sick, with coughs, colds, and flu, and won't be there that day.

I've written entire homework reports for my children. I feel safe admitting that only because you'll never guess which kid—

I have too many. And he *still* got a C minus. Yes, it was the blue whales one.

From time to time I write to the milkman, the pediatrician, the guy who delivers *The New York Times,* and the coordinator of my kids' school's cookie committee for the annual bake sale.

I love my life. I hate it too, sometimes. Getting to write about it is a wonderful thing. Very therapeutic. The kids keep it real. If you have them you know what I'm talking about.

And if you don't you might later. That's when the whole thing about the blue whales becomes obvious.

Doesn't it?

It might be time for my medication.

But when the publisher asked me what my book was about, it reminded me of the evening several years ago when my husband and I were sitting on the couch watching television and having a glass of wine.

The kids were in bed and for once we were not in the usual state of deep exhaustion bordering on comatose. Well, one thing led to another and we began to get a little frisky, as they say. It wasn't anything out of the Kama Sutra, mind you. We were simply two married people trying to see if eleven years of marriage was maybe too long.

That is, until we noticed our little six-year-old, Sammy, standing in the hallway staring at us. We made a haphazard attempt at recovery, ordered him back to bed, and sat there mortified, wondering what to do.

We discussed how to handle this delicate matter, and I was the one with the short straw, designated to go to his room and retuck him in. It was an effort to surreptitiously determine what he saw and how long he saw it.

I went to his room, pulled up his covers, tousled his hair, and gave him a good-night kiss. We chatted a little bit and he didn't say a word about what had just happened. I was *so* relieved. Then, as I got to the door, ready to slip away, he said, "Mom?"

"Yes, peanut?"

"What in the *world* were you two doing?" he asked.

"I have no idea," I said, shutting the door and running down the hall.

And that's also what I said to the publisher about this book.

But I hope you'll enjoy it. And, unlike some people we know, you won't require six months of therapy afterward.

At least I don't think so.

And if you do, well, what can I say?

It's my *first* book, after all.

CLEVE
LAND

MY CHILDHOOD:
WHERE DID IT ALL GO RIGHT?

I SUFFER FROM an early childhood malady that is more common than you've been led to believe. I call it Way Too Normal and Happy Upbringing Syndrome. Or, as *you* probably know it, WTNHUS. It's easier to say if you hold your nose closed really tight with your thumb and forefinger. Go ahead, I'll wait.

See, the problem is that I grew up in an average westside Cleveland suburb, in an average, fairly functional, devout Catholic family, two parents, different sexes, five kids, no divorce, suicide, sexual abuse, drug addiction, or jail time. We didn't have a lot of money but we weren't poor. We got to do cool stuff because our dad was a sportswriter, but we weren't rich either.

We lived in a tree-laden five-miles-long-by-two-miles-wide village on Lake Erie that was like Andy Griffith's fictional Mayberry. Minus the Barneys, Gomers, and Floyds. We did have a few Aunt Bees. It was the mid-sixties, and we were close enough to Cleveland to have cool music, professional sports, and tons of movie theaters. The Beatles, the Stones, Jimi Hendrix, and Barbra Streisand all made stops there. And we were far enough away from downtown to be able to read about local poverty and race riots like they were happening somewhere else.

Bay Village was such a soft, gentle community that the kids from the suburbs closer to Cleveland called it Gay Village. We could walk to the beach, ride bikes to our friends' houses, buy penny candy and lucky rabbits' feet from the five-and-dime. Every Fourth of July there were fireworks, a carnival, and a parade where we displayed the bikes we had decorated with red, white, and blue crepe paper in the spokes and pinwheels on the handlebars. My best friend across the street, Sally Greene, discovered that if you soaked the crepe paper in water it would color it, and suggested that we could make a killing if we put the colored water in jars and sold it—you know, colored-crepe-paper water. Oddly enough, no takers.

We picked elderberries by the railroad tracks, which permanently stained our moms' Formica countertops when we made them into pies. Four cups of sugar on those berries. (Count 'em, four.) We played Tag, Capture the Flag, Hide and Seek, Four Square, Red Light/Green Light, Hopscotch, Statues, Running Bases, and the ever-popular Whack the Lightning Bug (or fireflies, or whatever you call them where you live) with the Whiffle-Ball Bat. They were the only animals harmed in the writing of this book, by the way. Except when my cousin Art accidentally whacked me on the back in pursuit of a lightning-bug whacking record.

There were seven families on the end of the street (Midland Road, how average is that?), with a median of four kids per family. We ran in packs. Boys playing sports, girls singing the entire score from the movie *Mary Poppins* on the swing sets at Normandy School. (Well, me. I sang.)

We played for hours. Rules were in place. We had to be home when the streetlights came on. Or when Mom gave the whistle using her pinkie and forefinger that I have never been able to replicate.

Everyone had their share of accidents. When my brother and his cronies locked us girls out of our secret club in the garage and began to read our supersecret diaries, I put my fist through the garage door trying to get in. My dad went ballistic. I got a Band-Aid and was grounded, which at that time meant I couldn't go farther than our front steps. The girls brought me graham crackers.

Dicky Greene "accidentally" dropped a hammer from the top of a twenty-foot tree onto Johnny Madden's head. They were building a tree fort. (See, this was back when kids built their own tree houses; their parents didn't hire I. M. Pei to do it for them.)

Suzie Albertz with the long hair did a triple flip over the front of her handlebars as we careened down Huntington Hill. And lived! Cool!

Thor Johnson stuck his head through the glass window of our front storm door while chasing my brother, who was attempting to liberate the ants in his ant farm. This was *way* before PETA.

And throughout the years in a show of unity we all took turns getting stung by bees, stepping on broken glass, and stubbing our toes on uneven suburban sidewalks when we weren't skinning our knees while roller-skating (no helmets, no wrist guards—all you needed was a skate key and guts, baby).

For years we would Stay in Bay All Day. We went sledding in the winter and swimming all summer. We went to church on Sundays and had Dairy Queen every chance we got. It was all pretty midwestern-romantic. Ohio has all four seasons in a very big way. There were entire weeks we missed school because of snow. Not that we *missed* it exactly. And spring can't help but be luminous after those kinds of long winters. Summer was one long sun-scorched, barefoot blast, and there's nothing quite so spectacular as an Ohio autumn when the leaves are turning. No hallucinogens necessary.

There was a lot of laughter in our house. I remember nights when the five of us were all at the dining room table *not* doing our homework. Just laughing and laughing. Well, not always laughing. My sister Alice and I fought constantly, and one night she lured me into the basement and, on a dare, threw an entire chocolate-frosted pound cake at me that was intended for the school bake sale. Some *pound* cake—that mother knocked me right up against the cement-block wall. I had frosting in my ears for a week.

There was and probably still is just something damn lovable about unpretentious, wise-guy, hangdog Cleveland. If there was ever a place that is proud if its own, that cheers on its children, that takes great parochial offense at even the hint of a slight, Cleveland is that place. The town has some faults: it's got an enormous inferiority complex (the river caught on fire), and geographic racial segregation second only to South Africa.

But that place is always in my heart. If you're from Cleveland and you do something good, those people will love you forever. In fact, they'll love you even if you're just passing through. Tom Hanks spent one summer there in the seventies, watching the Indians while he was working at the Great Lakes Shakespeare Festival, and he's considered a hometown boy.

Now, lest you think my life all too good to be true, my growing up was not without its very own "Movie of the Week" devastation. In 1971, when I was twelve, my mom had a brain aneurysm and died. Don't think that hasn't cost me a pretty penny in therapy over the years.

It's a bit rough getting a mortality wake-up call at that age. But it makes you realize that challenges, difficulties, and bad breaks are not the worst things that can happen to you. So later on, when you don't get that big part in the *Porky's* reunion movie, you still get that very real feeling of "Hell, at least I ain't dead!"

But what really irritates me are some people's two-bit analyses regarding showbiz folks and the drive for fame. I've been asked if my mother's death propelled me into the acting world, desperate for the love I lost.

I say *Ha!* When I was in the second grade at St. Raphael's, seven years before my mom died, I told Sister Delrina I could sing the entire *Color Me Barbra* album, and then proceeded to perform it, not only for my own class but for five others as well.

You want to blame someone for me being an attention-starved, "Look at me, look at me," messed-up, sociopathically needy showbiz person? The buck stops here, my friend. I'm *healthy*.

And I've got the childhood to prove it.

A BRIEF HISTORY OF
CLEVELAND

1796   Moses Cleveland and a survey party land at the mouth
       of the Cuyahoga River on July 22. No one involved
       imagined the river catching on fire, the city defaulting,
       the Browns leaving for Baltimore, or what one hundred
       fiercely subzero winters might be like.
           So they stayed.

1803   Ohio is admitted to the Union. Thereby making
       Woody Hayes possible. Make your own call here.

1842   January 7, the Cleveland *Plain Dealer* newspaper begins
       publication. This allows my ancestors to shift the family
       business from horse *thievery* to horse puckey. I'm *kid-
       ding*, of course.

1847   The Catholic diocese is created. Religious leaders begin
       planning things for me to feel guilty about.

1861   Abraham Lincoln visits Cleveland. During his speech
       he never hints at the fact that I might be born here and

go on to win not one but two Emmy Awards. You have to admit the guy is somewhat overrated.

1916　The first production of the Cleveland Playhouse, members of which would later snub me when at the age of eleven I offered, by mail, to play the part of Juliet in their 1967 production of *Death of a Salesman*.

1950　The village of Bay (Bay Village) is incorporated as a city. I would be born there only eight years later and, with the help of the Sam Sheppard murder case in 1954, help put it on the map.

1956　My brother Michael is born. He would later spell-check this entire book *and* number the pages.

1958　I am born on March 4, found by my family floating in a basket among the reeds along the banks of the Cuyahoga River. Huzzahs are heard all around.

1964　The Cleveland Browns win the NFL league championship, defeating the Baltimore Colts in an upset, 27–0. At the same time I hear my first Barbra Streisand album and am forever transformed.

1969　The Cuyahoga River catches on fire; I get my first zit. The city and I are both mortified.

1972　The first issue of *Cleveland* magazine is published. *I* was on the cover of said magazine in February 2002. The story was fabulous. The cover wasn't all that flattering. Not that it's always all about *me*, mind you. But *that* issue was.

1978　Cleveland becomes the first major city to default on its financial obligations since the Depression. The exact same year I'm finally able to drink liquor legally and have *no* obligations! *Yeehaw!*

1980   I move from Cleveland to New York. (I'm not really all that sure what happened to Cleveland after that.)

1995   I read somewhere that Cleveland got the Rock and Roll Hall of Fame and Museum. But, sadly, I'm not in it. *Yet.*

1996   Cleveland celebrates its bicentennial. I think I was doing a road-show production of *Godspell* in Weehawken, New Jersey. I played Mary Magdelene's slutty friend Fuhdwa.

2002   Cleveland's great, I'm great. No worries. Not in the Rock Hall yet. That *still* kind of bugs me.

SURVIVAL JOBS:
PART I

PROBABLY A LARGE PART of my refusal to give up pursuing a life in show business is due not to my unbridled imagination, my singing voice, my ability to tap into my emotions on a dime (or for a dime), and certainly not my looks; it's due to my willingness to take any and every job to make a buck on the way there.

It started young, this need to work. Chores were my first taste of getting paid for something. And we actually had to complete an activity for the fifty cents a week.

Unlike *my* kids.

I've tried to start this chore business a million times, but it's so damn inconvenient. If I insisted that they make their beds before school every morning, we'd all have to either get up at five A.M. or just skip classes that day. And since I've become a member of the funny-monied and have a nanny and a housekeeper to do my job for me, I have to resort to exotic chores for my kids, like having them search the Internet to find Dad's Marmite, or organize Mom's nail polish.

My mother didn't have a housekeeper, and she had her hands full with the five of us, so there was plenty left over for us to do. Saturday mornings we had to dust, vacuum, and clean the bathrooms. My brother was assigned the more manly chores of taking out the garbage and mowing the lawn. I remember my brother complaining occasionally, but I never minded the housework. I found it interesting. I liked spraying Pledge all over the woodwork and watching it come up shining (just like in the commercials!). There was a sense of accomplishment in getting the ring out of the toilet bowl.

Even today, the first thing I do when I break for hiatus from the show is clean. I redo the linen closets, my closets, the kids' closets. I vacuum everything. I sort the Legos by color into little plastic bags. I'm a maniac. But it gives me a sense of accomplishment that's different and more immediate than being a TV actress.

All the girls in my neighborhood shared my affliction. We liked to keep busy, accomplish stuff, and get paid for it. Lemonade stands, live theatrical performances in my garage, street fairs—anything for a buck.

It wasn't always about money for me. Summers could get pretty boring in Bay Village, and one year, when I was twelve, I signed up to work as a volunteer at a summer school for kids with Down's syndrome. Now, part of me was just a do-good brownnoser, but I have also always had a heart for the mentally handicapped; some of my friends' siblings were mentally retarded. And I know they're gonna be about eight rungs above me in heaven and in charge of whether I get to fly, so I wanted to score a few points with them in this life. I had never had any experience working with any kind of kids before, so this was really diving into the deep end. Along with being a teacher's aide, I was the bus monitor for the kids' ride home. By the end of the morning I was exhausted. I lasted one summer. Enough brownie points.

Throughout elementary school I made a little pocket change addressing envelopes for our next-door neighbor, an optometrist who ran his business out of his house. I've always loved handwriting, and I used to practice different styles to keep it interesting. To this day, I can remember the zip codes for every west-side suburb of Cleveland.

At the end of my sophomore year in high school, I switched from an all-girls Catholic academy to my local public high school. This necessitated supplementing my wardrobe, which consisted of white blouses and blue herringbone skirts, knee-socks and saddle shoes. As the new girl, I needed to make a big impression. I needed polyester high-waisted bell-bottoms in pastel colors and matching sweaters accented with neck scarves. Think Cher meets Mary Tyler Moore. And kicks her ass.

This meant cash, and lots of it. Casual Corner was not cheap. Not to me. So I bicycled across town, sans helmet in heavy traffic, to the mall and secured a job at Halle's Department Store. I quit cross-country track to do this. Which was a questionable decision, because the result was that I became fat *and* wore bad clothes. And I have the yearbook photos to prove it.

But working at Halle's really helped to develop my independence. I overcame my fear of cash registers, and became quite adept at arranging the Monet jewelry in the display case. I worked in the women's department, so I was always the first among my friends to have the latest bad seventies fashion— with a 10 percent discount! At Christmas I got to help clueless men pick out outfits for their wives as gifts. It's amazing how men don't know a damn thing about the size of their women or what they like to wear. Every guy who came in said his wife or girlfriend was about my size. *Every guy.*

Occasionally I substituted in the handbags department, and one time I had one of the few bad experiences of my survival-job days. It involved an irate customer returning a purse. This broad was *angry,* and decided to vent it all on the sixteen-year-old dorky handbag-department substitute. She wanted to exchange her bag, and every time I showed her something else, she spat fire with "No, not *that* one!" Each bag I suggested made her angrier until I was sure she would tear my head off. She made me feel so worthless and stupid, I started to cry silently while I filled out her credit-card receipt, dripping tears onto the counter. That shook her up. She suddenly became shamefaced and couldn't get out of there fast enough.

I continued to take jobs through college too. I got a loan that paid for the tuition, but I still needed cash for books and beer. The first couple of weeks my roommates and I got wind of a great way to make a quick twenty-five bucks—selling plasma. As in our own plasma. As in going down to the clinic and sitting in a chair with a needle in our arms while the nurse extracted blood, spun the plasma out of it, and put our blood back in, all in the space of an hour. No experience necessary. After becoming plasma-less, we headed right out to High Street and became legless.

But there was a limit to how often you could sell your body, at least certain parts of it, so I needed to find a more legit source of income. I got a job dishing out the glop at my dorm's commissary. If you can call it legit—some of that food was unfit for human consumption. Once, while working in the back taking the dirty trays of dishes off the conveyer belt, we surmised that the spaghetti must have been overcooked. We deduced this from the message spelled out on one plate in green peas: "This tastes like s--t." Other dissatisfied students were less articulate—they merely mushed the pasta together along with anything else they could find on the table: salt and pepper, ketchup, their Psychology 101 final.

Working in the cafeteria was a great way to meet guys. Although the ones who showed any interest tended to be a little desperate, since I was chubby, wore an apron, and topped it all off with a hairnet. I must have had a winning smile.

I moved up a notch my junior and senior years of college when I became a waitress at the Faculty Club. We wore uniforms (no hairnets), and folded real cloth napkins. I discovered there are many ways to fold a napkin—the Bishop's Mitre, the Fleur-de-Lys, and the classic Fan. This was some of the most useful knowledge I gained at Ohio State University; I've used this skill to great advantage in restaurants in New York and even at my own dinner parties. I've yet to employ anything I learned in political science.

Let's not forget the six-week stint I had as an Ohio State

traffic controller. I needed money to pay for my membership in the Delta Gamma sorority, and traffic director fit all my requirements—decent money, few hours, and a Day-Glo vest and hat that really helped to accent the extra twenty pounds I was carrying.

The guy in charge of the student traffickers was a dead ringer for the Robert Duvall character, Kilgore, in *Apocalypse Now*—he took his job very seriously. I could tell by the smirk on his face that he didn't think I would last very long. He laid out the rules, the most important one being that you couldn't be late for work: not ten minutes, not five minutes, not five seconds. You had to be there when the van left to take you to your post.

Unfortunately, being late was a chronic problem for me all through my teens and twenties. Not sure what that was about, but there it was. Add to that I used to stay out late and drink a lot—old Robert Duvall knew one when he saw one. I did okay for a while, and had a good time making all those crabby morning-rush-hour drivers do whatever I wanted with a little flourish from my Day-Glo wands.

But those keggers have a way of catching up with you, and after six weeks and two late notices, Robert Duvall fired my butt. Interestingly, that six weeks' pay was just enough to cover my sorority dues and room and board; funny how I ran outta gas at the same time that I had fulfilled my financial obligation.

But the best part of all these jobs was the great people I met while struggling to get through. They were always crazy with a great sense of humor. The busboys at the Faculty Club insisted on being called the bus dudes; they felt it conferred more dignity upon the job. Patrick, the tallest Irish waiter I've ever met, and Deb, the tiniest Jewish waitress I've ever met, met over the sticky-bun warming drawer and have been together ever since. The only thing that happened to me as a result of the sticky-bun warming drawer was an extra fifteen pounds.

Of course, one always encounters the odd jerk or two at these places. Some are resentful and bitter because they know we part-timers are just passing through and don't consider these jobs real work, while they, the higher-ups, are stuck for life. Others are just overinflated bombasts with a misplaced sense of self-importance.

Like a newscaster I worked for at the ABC-TV affiliate in Cleveland. My dad secured me a summer job developing and editing footage for the local news. I knew nothing about it, so I worked my butt off to learn, coming in early to practice loading the magazines with film in the darkroom and running it through these big, ancient developing machines. After I learned that, I graduated to actually cutting and pasting the news stories together. This was in the old days, before digital cameras and computerized editing, and once you made a cut in the film, there was no turning back.

One weekend a bunch of the people in the newsroom called in sick, and I, the know-nothing summer intern, was stuck with developing, editing, and loading the whole damn six o'clock news, plus running the TelePrompTer. There was some story about a boating accident on Lake Erie, and the only shot the lame camera guy got was of a dinghy bobbing up and down on the water. I edited the piece as best I could: the dinghy from the right, the dinghy from the left, behind the dinghy, in front of the dinghy. I was frantic all day trying to do everything myself and scared poopless.

But at six-thirty, when the news had successfully finished, the other loser weekend intern and I whooped with relief. Just then I get a call from the weekday anchor. Let's call him Ward Buttley. Ward Buttley was straight out of central casting: tall, thin, big fake teeth, big sprayed hair, a married guy having an affair with Peggy, one of those smart-but-dumb-about-guys chicks, who worked at the station. Ward had just watched our broadcast from his armchair at home, and was furious with our dinghy footage, blaming me for picking bad shots. He screamed at me for ten minutes over the phone, threatening to have my job. The next morning he stormed in and made me sit down next to him as he looked at all the dinghy footage we hadn't used. After scrolling through ten minutes of an empty Lake Erie, he smiled his best cheesy-newscaster smile and said sweetly, "Well, I guess you used the best footage you had. Sorry about that." He gave me a big wink and left the editing bay. What a *jerk*.

However, I must thank Ward Buttley. It's people like him who made me want to get far away from crap like that and spend my life doing what I love to do. The jerks and the creeps are just as much a part of the whole process as the wild crazies are. I thank them all.

Because there were plenty more to come.

THE DEAN OF AMERICAN
SPORTSWRITERS

PEOPLE WHO KNEW ME WHEN often ask if it's difficult for me to handle the fame and fortune that's come my way. I tell them that it's all surreal, I never could have imagined it, and I'll never get used to it.

All lies.

The fact is I've been well prepared for success. I became accustomed to the fame, if not exactly the fortune, and all the perks that go along with being a celebrity, because I grew up with one—my dad the sportswriter.

Cleveland is famous for being a football town, even with the Browns leaving and then being reconfigured and all that mess. But back in the day, after they won the NFL championship in 1964 and on through the Kardiac Kids era in the 1970s and beyond, there was an unparalleled purity of devotion to the Browns by the people of Cleveland that only a handful of American cities know. And all throughout that time Chuck Heaton was one of the major daily connections between Browns fans and the football team they loved.

Today, even at the age of eighty-four, my dad still looms large in the hearts and minds of generations of Clevelanders. He was the first famous person I ever knew. The players great (Jim Brown) and small (Walt "The Flea" Roberts) were always the focus, but my dad was there, covering more than thirty years of Browns football. He epitomized the gentleman sportswriter of his era. He was smart and sharp and fair. He treated the people he covered and the people with whom he worked with dignity, kindness, and class. People *still* tell me that.

Growing up in Cleveland as his kid was a position of privilege. There was a certain grace that went along with being one of his children. If I had a nickel for every time somebody said in hushed tones, "Her dad's Chuck Heaton," I wouldn't need to work.

And speaking of work, the man damn near killed himself by providing for us. He was heroically hardworking. Besides writing three stories a day (a beat story, a column, and notes), during football season, which ran from the Fourth of July to the end of January, he was also a Cleveland correspondent for *Sports Illustrated, Pro Football Digest,* and two or three other publications.

He provided a roof, food, and clothes, and got five kids through Catholic schools and college. He is very much a man of his World War II generation: on the road a lot, and not especially touchy-feely or wise on the girl issues. But he is the dad who did right, and who was as good at home as he was in the hearts of the Browns' fans.

Now, all of this took awhile to dawn on me, of course. Because for the first few years of my life, I was a bit afraid of my dad. I mean, dads are generally at a disadvantage anyway in the initial stages of their kids' lives, because just the breast-feeding alone ensures that he will be second in line for affection for at least a year, and probably third or fourth in line if you figure in the binky and the applesauce.

And when I was growing up, Chuck, like most of the dads in our neighborhood, left early in the morning and came home after our dinnertime. So we didn't see him all day. On top of that, when he finally did come home, my mom left it to him to administer any spankings we had earned while he was out. Plus, we were expected to chill while he wound down from deadline pressure with a Jim Beam old-fashioned or two. Add to that the fact that Chuck was often on the road with the Browns or the Indians for days at a time, so it took me awhile to regard him as anything other than the great-but-distant provider.

But it didn't take long for me to start crawling up on his lap with my blanky to watch the nightly news with Huntley and Brinkley. Or to know that he just might have bull's-eye caramels in his pockets when he came through the door.

When we got a little older he'd take us downtown to the newspaper, where we would happily explore the office while he caught up on some work. Just the ride into the rugged industrial beauty of Cleveland was thrilling—not many kids I knew got to go into the city. And the Cleveland *Plain Dealer* was right out of *The Front Page*—men in shirtsleeves smoking cigarettes, tearing sheets of paper off the AP wire or sitting at their

Underwood typewriters in row upon row of desks shouting, "Copy!"

I loved it. The drawers in those desks held all kinds of mysterious treasures: rubber erasers that were sticky and stretchy, little metal and wood blocks of typeset, and red wax editing pencils that you sharpened by unwinding the string they were wrapped in. I knew my dad had a special job.

Especially when he took us to his other office—Cleveland Municipal Stadium. Grand and imposing, the stadium was the arena where great acts of glory and tragedy were played out. And everyone there knew my dad. From the fans waiting in line at the ticket booth to the cops in the parking lot to the elevator operator for the elite Stadium Club, shouts of "Hey, Chuck!" could be heard as we passed. And he always said "Hi" back. To everyone. He never lost that habit. To this day, every person whom he passes on his morning walk gets his jaunty "Howyadoin'?"

Being with my dad at these times made me feel important and special. We were allowed access to places where no one else we knew was—the Stadium Club, with its private elevator and Coca-Colas that were extra sweet and syrupy, poured by a real bartender; the press box, cramped and cold and lined with phones and more typewriters; and even, on occasion, the owner's box, where Art Modell and his glamorous wife, Pat, presided over the festivities.

Two weeks every summer Dad took us to the Browns' training camp at Hiram College. There is probably not a less exciting place on the planet, and yet I wouldn't have traded it for the French Riviera. Our family was housed in two tiny rooms behind the university cafeteria, just up the hill from the football field, a big Dumpster right outside the door—paradise.

We would spend the days running around the field's track, scaling the training equipment, and climbing up and down the bleachers. We'd watch the practices and the exhibition games, and my brother, the prince, got to be the water boy and hang out in the locker room.

The most exciting part of Hiram was the meals. We ate with the players, watching with fascination and awe as they loaded their plates in the cafeteria with steak, eggs, waffles, burgers, and usually two or three glasses of milk. As we sat and ate, the players put the rookies through their initiation— singing songs, dressing up, and doing skits. We knew we were witnessing something no mere commoner was allowed to see. These men—Jim Brown, Lou Groza, John Wooten, Bill Glass— were great mountains of muscle, their voices loud and confident. They towered over my dad, yet always deferred to him as if he were a visiting dignitary. They made a special point of talking and joking with "Chuck's kids." I liked this celebrity thing.

A gig like this could go to a guy's head. But not Chuck.

He may have had quite a presence in Cleveland, and I always jumped at the chance to tell people who my dad was, but there were other things about him that left an impression too. Like his monthly sit-down at the dining room table with the checkbook, where, after paying all the bills, he would then write out checks to the Maryknoll Missions, Father Flanagan's Boys Town, and any other Catholic organization that put the arm on him.

He was always trying to help someone else in trouble, even if it was just by getting them some free football or baseball tickets to pick up their spirits.

And despite all the hoopla connected with his job, he really wasn't making that much jack, but he still managed to take us out to dinner every one or two months and to the movies (with popcorn and drinks) every other week. He even sat through those interminably long Disney musicals, which I knew he abhorred.

Dad inherited a bit of an anxious nature from his mother. He was a big worrier about money and was known to lose his cool occasionally. That didn't stop him from hauling us on a family vacation every summer: driving for hours in an unair-conditioned sedan with seven people, dealing with the carsickness, bickering, and weird roadside attractions that are an essential part of July and August madness.

I guess it's that madness that keeps you going as a parent. Dad had it. You knew it when he'd wake you in the morning with a strange little ditty that began "Oh, they don't wear pants where Patty does her dance!" And later, when he went on a low-cholesterol diet and started running four miles every morning, he'd get us out of bed by taking off his smelly, sweaty T-shirt and threatening to rub it in our faces.

He'd come down to breakfast, call my mom a "chubby rascal," and give her a cuddle. Over cereal he'd ask us, "Was it fair for God to make one man so handsome?"

He always had slightly off-color jokes that he collected for his speeches at father-son Communion breakfasts: The little boy who asked his first-grade teacher, a nun, if she knew why the ocean roared. "Well, Sister, you'd roar too if you had crabs on your bottom."

He saved the more off-color jokes for his Touchdown Club talks. There was the one about the Cleveland Browns player whose wife complained that he was too uncouth. He responds by saying, "We eat in nice restaurants, don't we? We go to the theater, don't we?" She says yes, they do. "So, what's this *uncouth* shit?"

As my sisters started going off to college, the family activities died down a bit, and Dad got worn-out a bit too. He didn't always make it to my choir concerts, and he lost his temper more often when the teenage years worked their magic on my siblings.

Around this time my mom died, and everything became just this side of weird. Especially my dad's "dating" period. It consisted of one or two dates with each of the widows in our parish. Unfortunately for him, I was doing community theater musicals at the time, and he was forced to sit through a three-hour (bad) production of *Showboat* about eight times while looking for his future bride.

She turned out to be Cece Evers, and they've recently celebrated their twentieth wedding anniversary. It was an uneasy adjustment at first, and Cece bore the brunt of it. Lovingly and heroically. To this day she is my dad's heart and soul. And we love her so much for it. Back then it wasn't easy. We all just soldiered along, and maybe that period of emotional pain is what prompted my move to New York.

I announced to Dad at dinner a few weeks after graduating from Ohio State that I was heading out to Manhattan. He told me no, and for the first time I defied him: "I'm not asking you, Dad. I'm telling you." Instead of the angry outburst I expected, he just said "Okay" and asked how much I needed to make the move.

After that, he always tried to talk me into coming back home, offering to find me a job in Cleveland at a bank or a TV station. Even when I called him to say I had gotten a part in a Broadway musical, he said, "Maybe when it's over you can move back." But he came and saw the show, and one other off-off effort I produced, and didn't even let his cringe show when he saw the dumpy studio apartment I was living in.

When I finally did get my first sitcom, Dad sent me a letter. It wasn't the first time he'd written, but it was the first time he told me how proud he was of me and all that I had accomplished. I sat in the stairwell of our little apartment and cried my eyes out. My husband had never seen me like that before.

It was that kind of thing that sticks with me about Dad. He didn't always know the right thing to do, but he made a stab at it. Like the time I went through a mid-teen crisis.

When I was sixteen I became mysteriously plagued with headaches and nausea. Since my mom's death was from a brain aneurysm, Dad took me to the Cleveland Clinic to get checked out. They couldn't find anything and told my dad I was depressed.

On the way home he stopped at some hip clothing boutique of the day, J. P. Snodhoppers or something, and he bought me a pair of corduroy hip-huggers. This may not seem like much, but if you knew how totally removed my dad was from girls, clothes, and blowing money needlessly, you'd see what a sweet and touching gesture of love this was.

I'll never forget it and I'm sure he never gave it a second thought.

YEARNING AND LEARNING

I HAVE FOUR BOYS, and one of them has shown a distinct aversion to school and all things educational. This has caused me to spend more than a few nights tossing sleeplessly as I pondered his future. How was this kid ever going to make it?

I don't know about all of you out there in the real world, but here in Fairyland, the future of America is all tied up in what outrageously expensive elementary school your child attends.

This can be a problem if a) you're not outrageously rich, b) you're outrageously rich but your kid doesn't make the cut, or c) you're outrageously rich, your kid makes the cut, but he pitches a fit every morning because he doesn't want to go, and he refuses to do the work once you've dragged him into the classroom kicking and screaming, and he comes home every day with "Incomplete" written across the top of his papers.

What possible chance does a kid like that have?

I've heard of parents who have gone to great lengths and expense to get their kids into the crème de la crème of schools, and still send them to a tutor in the afternoons. There are a million extracurricular activities that are apparently de rigueur for a twelve-year-old's résumé if that child is to have a shot at anything other than being homeless or on welfare. Or so parents are told.

If that's the truth, then how did I get here?

There wasn't all this applying-to-schools business in the sixties, at least not where I'm from. In Ohio, you went to the school closest to where you lived. Period. No magnet schools, no academies, no gifted programs.

High school was the same. You had a choice of either public or parochial, and I had a taste of both. I spent the first two years at an all-girls Catholic academy, where my goal was to be the most popular. Being top of your class academically was not among the criteria. Being loud, funny, cute, obnoxious, and having a cool boyfriend—those were the things that mattered.

Activities at my all-girls Catholic high school included rolling my skirt, putting Jell-O into unsuspecting friends' purses, and cutting school to go downtown for the St. Patrick's Day parade.

When I switched to the public school in my junior year, my goal was to be the most popular. (See above criteria.) This included being on the drill team, the yearbook staff, and the pep club, and singing two solos with the jazz band. Not much time for academics. I was able to keep my grades up, but only because I have an excellent short-term memory, and cramming became a way of life for me.

It probably wouldn't have mattered what my grade-point

average was, because I ended up going to Ohio State, where the only requirements for acceptance were that you had to be breathing and carrying a number-two pencil.

When I wasn't partying, I was attending a number of classes that seemed to bear no relation to one another or to my major, which was originally journalism. After four years there, the only three classes I can remember are a logics course, which was taken on a computer, the tests of which you could take repeatedly until you got the grade you were looking for; the history of the Jews; and French. Not exactly a recipe for world domination.

I spent most of my time making midnight runs to White Castle in my pajamas with my sorority sisters, building floats, eating too much, drinking too much, and trying to lose weight.

And yet, today I'm doing okay. So, what gives? Do we really need to stuff our kids with quality time and quantities of activities? Is that what's going to make them successful human beings? And by the way, just how do we define a successful human being?

Let's take Albert Einstein. I think we could all agree that he was a fairly successful human being. He had a lovely family and made some valuable contributions to mankind. This same person didn't start speaking until way after his peers, causing his parents much consternation. He did poorly in school, quit for a while because he hated organized education, finally ended up with a teaching degree, couldn't find a job, and so worked in a patent office for seven years. No soccer camp, no cotillion, no SATs. Just a love of science.

And what about Dave Thomas, founder of Wendy's? Adoptive mother dies, he's left with a father who never speaks, and the two of them spend a lot of time eating silently in restaurants. Thomas drops out of high school and starts working at these same places, and later becomes one of America's greatest businessmen and philanthropists. No quality time, no field trips, just a love of food and business.

There is something about people as diverse as Albert Einstein and Dave Thomas. They really loved doing something, and they devoted themselves to doing the thing they loved. And they both had to overcome a lot to get there.

There are a lot of those kinds of stories about people in my business. So many of them struggled early on and for many years, and have succeeded because of their love of what they were pursuing. And the struggles have enhanced their art. And there are other important influences in their lives that have nothing to do with their formal education.

—

I'M REMINDED ABOUT how and why I first got excited about acting. And first it was the *movies*. Specifically, Shirley Temple movies. I wanted to *be* her. (My third son, Joe, said the same thing to me after he saw Bruce Springsteen on TV: "Mom, I'm *him*.")

The annual television presentation of *The Wizard of Oz*, without commercial interruption, was huge. From the time I was seven until I was seventeen I saw that movie every year. For us it was like a holiday. Thanksgiving, Christmas, Easter, and *The Wizard of Oz*.

But there were other life-altering cinematic events.

Unforgettable musicals, like *The Sound of Music*, *The Music Man*, *West Side Story*, and *The King and I*.

As I got older, there were dramas: *Days of Wine and Roses*, *To Kill a Mockingbird*, and *On the Waterfront*. The comedies, like *It's a Mad Mad Mad Mad World*, *The Russians Are Coming! The Russians Are Coming!*, and *The Pink Panther*, had my mother in tears of laughter.

Those were big movies with important themes that had an impact on my young mind. They explained the world and made me want to see more of them (the movies) and it (the world).

When my big sister Alice got involved in Community Theater in Cleveland it was life-changing for *me*. I became aware that the magic made by these movie actors on the big screen began at one time somewhere in the real world in small theaters.

Alice is a talented actress and a true artist. Six years older than me, Alice would practice her monologues for us younger siblings and perhaps visiting neighborhood friends. Standing alone in our artificially darkened living room, she could believably re-create Amanda Wingfield, the mother in Tennessee Williams's play *The Glass Menagerie*.

I remember her doing the scene when Momma finds out that her crippled daughter, Laura, the only person who might separate her from a life of poverty and humiliation, hasn't been going to her typing classes all these weeks and months. It was powerful.

And it was my dumb big sister Alice, who I fought with all the time, who suddenly transformed herself into this Southern matriarch. Somewhere, even at the age of ten or eleven, I made the connection between what Alice was doing and what I was seeing on the big screen. It was called *acting*.

And it was that Tennessee Williams monologue which won my sister a prestigious Martha Holden Jennings scholarship from the Cleveland Playhouse to attend an acting workshop in New York City the summer between her junior and senior years in high school. She might as well have been an astronaut selected to go to the moon as far as we were concerned.

It was a big deal. And not something that happened in every family on our street. Alice was also in plays at Huntington Playhouse, our local community theater. She was in *Bye Bye Birdie*, *West Side Story*, and *MacBird* (a political satire about LBJ). All of these experiences, while they became less extraordinary over time, slowly must have implanted the idea in my mind that acting was something I could do.

Another seminal experience, and really bizarre when I think back on it now, was the night our mom took the whole family to some far-flung east-side Cleveland suburban high school auditorium to see the Swedish actress Viveca Lindfors do Strindberg monologues.

Here's why this was especially weird. My mom was no slouch in the brains department. She was deep intellectually. But her areas were theology and socially concerned politics. She was not especially a *fine arts* gal. So what the hell were we doing at this rare performance of a foreign actress doing Strindberg's and Chekhov's greatest hits?

Perhaps Mom recognized something cool and obscure when it hit the hinterlands. Or was it that Lindfors had played Mary in the 1961 *King of Kings*, starring Jeffrey Hunter as Jesus?

I'll never know. But I'll never forget it either. Again, this was *acting*. And the not-so-subliminal message was that people did it for a living. Perhaps the most important information (and something I missed at the time) was that famous Swedish actresses who had starred in big Hollywood films still found it necessary to do one-woman shows in high school auditoriums in Middleburg Heights, Ohio, to pay bills between gigs. I have so much to look forward to.

But I followed Alice into Huntington Playhouse when I performed in the choruses of *Showboat* and *Bells Are Ringing*. I also began doing high school shows: *Oliver!* and *Fiddler on the Roof*. I started "trodding the boards," as they say. In the suburbs we called it "boring the trods," and it means exactly what it sounds like.

When it came time for college I really didn't know what I was doing and went into a kind of sensible cruise-control mode, choosing journalism as a major when I had very little interest in it.

Choral singing kept my performing bug alive through the first two years of college. But then it dawned on me that I was missing my own big picture. I was dying to be an actress. I was worried that my dad might be mad, but I changed my major to drama.

He told me to do what made me happy. And it's made me very happy. It's also caused me to think about how to encourage my kids in their life development.

I've decided not to worry so much about school and grades, because I'm not so sure about schools as they apply toward paving the way to success. There seems to be this belief that if you have enough jack you can put your kid on a paid-for path. And that success, riches, and happiness will follow.

It doesn't always work that way. True, kids can grow up with every educational, social, and economic privilege available and become model human beings—productive, fulfilled, and a benefit to society. Or they can become lazy, spoiled, self-indulgent losers. The exact same thing can be said for someone growing up in difficult circumstances.

So I've come to the conclusion that the main reason a person ends up where she does is because it's hardwired into her system in the womb. Those who break through whatever their circumstances are have two things that set them apart.

The first thing is talent. You either got it or you don't.

Know what's even more important than talent?

Desire.

It comes from many places in the heart. When strong it overcomes all else. It confers destiny. If you want to spend the rest of your life doing something you enjoy, it's all about desire.

Some people possess that desire from the beginning. They know that there's something out there that they have to be a part of. For others it takes some kind of epiphany, a watershed experience to awaken their dream. Many doctors started on their road because an illness in their family spurred them on to be a part of the cure.

For me, it was the first time I sang "The Itsy Bitsy Spider" for my Aunt Jane and got applause.

Laurence Olivier described it like this: "If I wasn't an actor, I think I'd have gone mad. You have to have extra voltage, some extra temperament, to reach certain heights."

That's a pretty elegant way of saying "Look at me, look at me, look at me."

Which is pretty much what I am about. I used to say that to my mom all summer long, each time I jumped off the diving board at the local pool. The *low* diving board. And I did it a thousand times a day. Still, the refrain was the same: *"Look at me!"*

So I'm just looking for the signs in my little guys, trying to figure out not what school they should get into but just what world they should get into.

My little Bruce Springsteen admirer seems to have a touch of the desire to perform. My oldest has quite an entrepreneurial spirit, and my youngest is just a plain menace to society. So, what about the one who hates school?

I found his school newspaper in his backpack. In his class's section, the students could write about either their field trip or the Easter bunny. Most of the class wrote things like "We went to the museum. We saw dinosaurs. It was fun." Or "The bunny put my eggs in a basket."

Here's what my guy wrote:

FLOWERS
by John Hunt

Flowers grow
In the grass.
Pretty, sweet flowers
In my garden.

I'm sleeping better already.

MY TELEVISION FAMILY VERSUS
MY REAL FAMILY

REAL FAMILY
1. My real family *really* loves me.
2. My real family is always there for me.
3. I gave birth to my own kids.
4. The kids go so far as to look like me.
5. My real family doesn't care if I'm on TV or not. As long as the money keeps rolling in.
6. My real family doesn't have to remember my birthday.
7. Twenty years down the road, if the whole thing goes to hell, somebody in my family will have a couch I can sleep on.
8. They really know me. And still talk to me.
9. They are *always* there for me.
10. My real family will remember me fondly on the day of my funeral.

TV FAMILY
1. My TV family doesn't really love me but is good at faking it.

2. My TV family is only there for me Monday through Thursday for twenty-six weeks a year. Or until cancellation.

3. Other people gave birth to my kids.

4. None of them look remotely like me.

5. My TV family likes that I'm on their TV show. As long as the money keeps rolling in.

6. Their assistants have to remember my birthday.

7. If the whole thing goes to hell, we'll all be on someone else's couch—most likely our shrinks'.

8. They don't know me at all, and will tell me any crazy damn thing.

9. My TV family is always there for me, except if they need to take a call on their cell, in which case if it's their agent, I'll have to tape up my slashed wrists myself.

10. My TV family will remember me fondly on the E! network's "Tragic Hollywood Death Bio Special," which will run forever.

MY ULTIMATE SIXTIES CHILDHOOD
EXPERIENCE

I REMEMBER IT like it was thirty-six years ago. Which it was. Which is to say I don't remember it all that well. But enough. I was eight years old that Sunday afternoon and sick with the flu. I remember that because I got out of going to mass in the morning and wore my pink fuzzy bathrobe all day.

There was a lot of excitement in the house that afternoon. Nervous excitement. We were having company. And normally we didn't have much company. My parents weren't all that social at home. Twice a year, at Christmas and Easter, we'd have Aunt Jane, my dad's sister, and Uncle Ed over for dinner. That was about it.

But this Sunday in 1966 the Negroes were coming. A black couple from East Cleveland was coming over to have dinner at our house. It was part of a program at church to help improve race relations and encourage support for the civil rights movement.

My mom had always been involved in the social issues of the day. We were against abortion, we were for the civil rights movement, we enthusiastically embraced the changes brought about in the Catholic Church by the Second Vatican Council. We voted Democrat (they were for helping poor people). We were against the war in Vietnam.

My mom's social and political beliefs were closely tied to her deep religious faith. She went to mass every day. She studied the writings of the Trappist monk Thomas Merton and the scientist-philosopher-priest Teilhard de Chardin. She also liked the novels of Graham Greene. I can still see the cover of the paperback version of *The Power and the Glory,* about the drunken priest in the third-world country. My dad read Ian Fleming.

So my mom, who was normally very easygoing (I think being one of fifteen children had something to do with that), was a bit tense. It wasn't about improving race relations that afternoon. It was about *initiating* race relations.

Cleveland was and is one of the most segregated cities in the United States. Where we lived, in Bay Village, the place was so homogenized we were considered exotic for being Catholic. There was one black family and one Jewish family in our town. Or so it was rumored. So this was sort of a big deal. Not everybody where we lived was crazy about the idea of Negroes coming out there for dinner.

In fact, some of my mom's brothers, who were real estate brokers, were kind of wishing she'd find another cause. They were worried about property values and once even approached my dad, asking if he could talk some sense into their sister. My dad, who knew a lot of black people from being a sportswriter, backed her 100 percent.

So there was a little extra tension besides the kind that normally comes with having company. The first sign of trouble erupted when my older brother, Michael, who was ten at the time, asked my mom if the company would be gone in time for us to watch the Beatles on *Ed Sullivan*.

My mom gathered all the kids together. "We are *not* watching the Beatles on *Ed Sullivan*," she told us in no uncertain terms. "We are going to be attentive and gracious and polite to our guests. We are going to be on our best behavior. Is that clear?" She was as serious as a heart attack. We nodded, but we were sulking. The Beatles were the biggest deal ever.

Our company arrived sometime near dinner. There was a cocktail hour planned so that our neighbors could come over and meet the black couple, which they did. It all sounds so awkward and earnest in retrospect. But admirable too, in a naïve way.

To us kids it was just another adult thing that was interfering with our fun. Did we think the world revolved around us and our desire for a good time? Yes, we did. We still do. We made the most of the adult cocktail hour by parading our new friends around to the rest of the kids in the neighborhood. We felt pretty cool and distinguished to have black friends, because nobody else did and it gave us a new status. Our house was the place where, finally, things happened.

Once the cocktail hour was over and the neighbors left, we

sat down to dinner with our guests. I don't remember their names, but the woman seemed much younger than her husband. And she was fun and vivacious. We probably had roast beef and potatoes because that was the kind of thing we had on Sunday nights.

After we said the world's longest Catholic grace before dinner, the conversation that followed was stilted and punctuated with uncomfortable pauses. There were polite questions and polite answers, but it was clearly a strained social situation. Once they got through sports and the weather (two minutes), everyone ran out of things to say.

Except for my brother Michael, the family cutup. Ever the one to rescue an awkward social moment, he announced that he knew a joke about a black boy, and did we all want to hear it? My mom almost choked on her carrots when the black woman said that yes, of course, she'd *love* to hear the joke. He told it like this, while my mom held her breath: "Once down in the country a white man came up to a colored boy and asked him if he'd like to buy some smart pills. The colored boy asked how much the smart pills cost. The white man said he would sell him five smart pills for a dollar. The boy agreed and gave the man a dollar and ate the smart pills. As soon as he ate them he complained to the man. "'These aren't smart pills,'" he said to the man. "'These are raisins.'" The white man smiled. "'See, boy,'" he said, "'you're smart already.'"

Everybody roared with laughter, including my mother, who I think was enormously relieved that the joke was mild and relatively inoffensive. But she quickly said with great decisiveness, "Okay, no more jokes," and shot my brother a look as if he had just donned a white sheet.

But my brother wasn't through. He then turned to the woman and said, "Did you know the Beatles are on *Ed Sullivan* tonight?"

The woman seemed genuinely surprised and delighted. "I had no idea," she said. "We *must* watch it." And then she looked at our mom, who joined right in with "Of course, we *must.*"

So out came the TV trays and we hauled the meal into the family room. This was a first for the Heatons because we *never* ate in front of the television. My mom was staring daggers at my brother, who was so happy about seeing the Beatles, he couldn't have cared less.

Once we got settled in, the tension and suspense of waiting for the Beatles to come on while the girls in the audience screamed like mad broke the ice. It was exactly what this poor gaggle of well-meaning Christians needed: some damn thing to talk about. Who knew that Ed Sullivan could be an instrument of God and a mediator of race relations? Watching Topo Gigio and the guy who spun the plates gave everybody something to talk about and took the pressure off everyone to save the world. Or at least America.

And when the Beatles finally did appear, my sisters screamed, my brother and I laughed at my sisters, and we all enjoyed the music. It was as if rock and roll via the Mop Tops had saved the Heaton family, the civil rights movement, and my brother from getting his backside tanned.

We never saw those people again. Race relations in this country still need to be improved, and my mom and two of the Beatles have since died. But for one evening in 1966 in Cleveland, Ohio, everything was as close to perfect as it was ever going to be.

RAISING KIDS/LOWERING
EXPECTATIONS

YOU KNOW, when my pediatrician looks at me straggling into his office with four kids in tow, I'm sure he thinks, "Job security!" I guess it's a big deal today to have four kids. But growing up in Cleveland, if you had only four kids it was assumed there were problems in the reproductive department.

Case in point: my grandmother had fifteen children and was named Catholic mother of the year for the United States and got a medal from the pope. When she went to Rome for the award ceremony, the pope kissed *her* ring.

It was great coming from a big family; you felt you really knew who you were. Although you didn't always know who your relatives were. I once picked up a hitchhiker in the Cleveland suburbs in the days when you could still pick up a hitchhiker and the chances of him being a homicidal maniac were only fifty-fifty. Anyway, he was cute and close to my age. The conversation went something like this:

"Where are you going?"

"Bay Village."

"Oh, I live in Bay Village."

"Yeah? My uncle lives in Bay Village. He's a sportswriter."

"My dad's a sportswriter. Chuck Heaton."

"He's my uncle! You're my cousin?"

"Guess so! Well, nice to meet you. Now, get out of the car. I'm turning here. And take your banjo with you."

Aaaanyway, parenting was very different for my mom and dad back then. Speaking of doctors, there were only two cures for every medical problem that went through the house: the flu was cured with ginger ale, saltines, and a bucket next to the bed; and for cuts and bruises, "Spit on it and rub." I don't remember *ever* going to the pediatrician's office.

Aside from the dentist, I rarely saw a doctor. Of the few times I did, the one that sticks in my mind is my first gynecological examination (at the age of eighteen, no less), where Dr. Sensitive's idea of helping me relax through the ordeal was to ask me whether I had had the steak or the lobster at the prom while he probed me with a speculum.

I mean, almost nothing warranted a doctor's visit. I actually fell from the top of a flight of stairs over the railing, bounced off my brother's Johnny Rebel cannon, and hit the cement floor of the basement with my head—no doctor's visit. When I put my fist through a plate-glass window I got a spanking and graham crackers—no doctor's visit. In order to win a trip to the doctor's office there had to be blood and plenty of it. You had to sever a major artery or suffer a head wound. Breaking a bone worked too.

The most contact I ever had with the medical world was

playing a gynecologist on the series *thirtysomething*. It was the first time I had ever heard the words *Pitocin* and *epidural*. Needless to say, I've become very familiar—even enamored—of those words, especially *epidural*. I *love* epidurals. I love scheduled C-sections, for that matter. Four blissful days in a hospital with painkillers, flowers, and no kids (except the baby, of course—the one the nurse brings to you only if you ring a bell for it). In fact, the reason I have four kids is not because I love children that much—it's because it's the only way I can guarantee four whole days to myself legally medicated.

But don't get me wrong. I love my kids. I can't imagine life without them. Our generation is probably a little too obsessed with their kids. I personally counted eighteen parenting guidebooks in my study, ranging from an Amish guide, which suggests using a switch by candlelight to keep the kids in line (and I suppose dressing them in black straw hats and making them pick up their dates in a buggy also dampens their spirits), to Penelope Leach, where you wait until your child is being led off in handcuffs before it occurs to you that letting him paint the cat when he was in the second grade might not have been the best way to express himself.

But I think my parents actually had the best idea—Catholic boot camp. It consisted of leaving books like *Lives of the Saints* lying around—full-color illustrations of Saint Sebastian tied to a tree with seventeen arrows in him and *still breathing*, or Saint Dymphna holding her eyeballs on a platter. That, plus firmly planting the idea of the reality of hell in her mind, will pretty much keep a kid in line for at least the first sixteen years.

We're probably too soft on kids these days. Despite my taking them to Sunday school every week and threatening them with eternal damnation, mine don't seem to have the same fear of God that I did. I overheard my two oldest talking one day about which one of them was stronger. John was saying, "I can hold the whole world in my hands." To which Sam replied, "Well, I can hold God in my hands." And John countered with, "Well, I can put Jesus on one finger and spin him!"

We worry so much about the effects of just about everything on our kids. My parents didn't seem that concerned. I'm always trying to sneak echinacea into their freshly squeezed, organically grown orange juice, while my mom was content to give us Pop-Tarts and Tang for breakfast. I've spent hours trying to convince my kids that a sugarless, flourless carob-chip cookie tastes as good as a double-stuffed Oreo, while my mom offered us a choice of three different artificial flavors of Space Food Sticks.

My mom was more concerned about our moral upbringing and what we read or watched on TV. She would cut out any offending articles or pictures in *Time* magazine (the issue featuring *Last Tango in Paris* was Swiss cheese), and we weren't allowed to watch *Peyton Place* (extramarital affairs), *Wild Wild West* (Robert Conrad's pants were too tight), or *Captain Kangaroo* (Mr. Green Jeans was suspected of growing nonunion grapes).

And today the big medical worries seem to be ear infections and the possible terrible long-term consequences of antibiotics. When I was growing up, the only constant medical problem seemed to be pinworms. Pinworms is that lovely childhood affliction where putting dirty fingernails in your mouth results in vermin up your bum. You know those cute pictures of kids with one arm twisted around behind them pulling at their underpants? Pinworms. Well, apparently I never washed my hands and always had my thumb in my mouth, because I had to drink that horrible red pinworm medicine at least three times a year. I don't remember that much from my childhood, but I do remember puking that stuff into a woven rattan wastepaper basket and watching helplessly as it splashed all over my slippies. (There's a way kids plaintively yell "Mom" that lets you know instantly that they've thrown up.)

I recently called my pediatrician, Dr. Bob, to ask him if one of my boys needed pinworm medicine. Now, according to Bob, kids rarely get pinworms anymore. I don't know what he was implying about where I grew up—I mean, I know it's Cleveland, and even though the city's motto is "At Least We're Not Akron," it's not exactly Appalachia. So I let the insult slide and listened intently as Bob told me that the best way to check for pinworms is to wait until the child is asleep, then take a flashlight, pull his cheeks apart, and look for the mother worm, which usually emerges at night. Pediatric humor at its finest.

Of course I fell for it. You know those people who have recovered memories of their parents forcing them to participate in satanic rituals? It was just their moms looking for pinworms.

Life was simpler in Cleveland. Parents were expected only to feed, clothe, house, and educate their kids. Today you're supposed to raise their self-esteem, give them piano and tae kwon do lessons, and teach them to download research for their kindergarten report on "My Family Tree—the Early Roman Years."

Add to that the fact that we're raising them in Hollywood. I'm suffused with guilt for working, so I'm smothering them with attention. Plus stuff. Lots of stuff. Hopefully they'll reject their mother's suffocating love and her rampant consumerism and live in a caring commune in Joshua Tree canning pickled cactus and meditating for world peace. Or it could all backfire and they could end up fat, spoiled slobs living off their trust funds while their sixty-year-old mommy tries to supplement her inadequate actor's pension by doing mattress commercials that air between midnight and three A.M.

Of course, I exaggerate. But I do have to compete with showbiz excess on a daily basis. Everyone becomes infected with showbiz excess. It's not just actors and producers who throw outrageous birthday parties. I've seen "normal" parents hire the second-stringers from Cirque de Soleil and have birthday cakes with more tiers than the one at my wedding. In Cleveland, when I grew up, no one thought it was necessary to have a lot of extras at our birthday parties—we would put Grandma in the middle of the room and play Spin the Wattle. Then, Find Dad's Partial, followed by Get the M&M Out of Baby Frannie's Nose.

Now, I'll admit it—I've hired party entertainers. I'll tell ya, it keeps an actor humble. To see an overweight forty-five-year-old guy in a shrink-wrapped Power Rangers suit, sweating out the previous night's case of Old Milwaukee, get out of his 1982 Honda Civic hatchback carrying a boom box to do funny noises and balloon animals for fifty bucks an hour makes me realize one thing: I should have charged more when *I* was doing it.

What I do like about L.A. are the numerous distractions for kids. When I watch them splash in the pool in January I realize that we have it so much easier now than when our family suffered through the deep, dark, snowy midwestern winters of Cleveland. It was like something out of *The Shining*. Indoors for months on end, my mother driven to insanity by the constant wail of "There's nothing to do!" and "I'm booored." The struggle to get our fat Pop-Tart and Velveeta-cheese bodies into huge puffy snowsuits and cover our shoes with Wonder bread bags before putting them into vulcanized-rubber snow boots, only to have us return five minutes later needing to go to the bathroom and demanding hot chocolate.

But winter did have its charms. Like Johnny Madden's yard. Johnny lived next door to us in a ranch house on a triple lot. In the winter, the neighborhood boys would construct a massive snow fort with two floors, a secret entry, and a special place to keep a supply of snowballs to ward off intruders. They taught us that if you put a rock inside the snowball, it was much more effective. And how. We'd race home from school to get an hour of snow-fort time in before it got dark.

Cleveland seemed like Sweden that way—in the winter, the sun went down at about two in the afternoon. I was immune to the cold then; even when my wrists had turned icy-hot red from where all the snow got in because I was wearing last year's too-small jacket, I played until just before the hypothermia did any permanent damage.

So I am a bit sorry that my kids don't get to experience the snow. Or the fall. We do get the occasional changing tree here, but not like in the emerald necklace of Cleveland. Or in

Johnny Madden's yard. Because as great as his yard was in the winter, it was even better in the fall. The twenty oak trees became gloriously ablaze with color before showering their leaves down upon us. And Mrs. Madden never had to pay anyone to rake them. We'd all come running with rakes from our garage and make a ten-foot-tall leaf pile that would be the source of our amusement for the next two weeks.

The best game in the fall was the Blanket Toss. A big, woolly old blanket was laid on the ground, and one of us girls would get in it. Both ends were tied, and then two of the boys would each pick up an end and start swinging. On the count of three the blanket was heaved onto the top of the leaf pile, and the passenger inside had to get free, Houdini-like, and find her way out. I'd lie there for a few minutes and just breathe in the lovely, musty leaf smell before crawling out from under the pile, my hair a tangle of leaves and branches.

My kids can get some of this in L.A., if we're willing to drive a few hours up to the mountains, which we're not. And until recently, the places where we lived had no yard whatsoever. And besides, the kids are never left outside alone. There's always a parent or nanny standing guard. I can't imagine one of my parents standing guard out in Johnny Madden's yard in the dead of winter while we made snow angels. So it breaks my heart when I tell my kids to go out and play and they ask, "But who's gonna watch us?"

What a different world I grew up in. Cleveland still takes its share of unfair knocks from people who have never been there. Like every place else it has its problems, but it can be a cool place to raise a bunch of healthy, happy, and relatively normal kids. And just like everywhere else these days, Cleveland has changed irrevocably due to the times in which we live. Still, it may be the closest thing to Mayberry you're ever going to find.

So while I'm here in Los Angeles providing job security for my pediatrician by having all these kids, I'd like to know where I could get a little security raising them. I suppose I should focus on the positive aspects of L.A.

We do have the ocean only twenty minutes away in one direction, and the mountains forty-five minutes in another. The climate is temperate all year, and the desert is one of the most magical places in the world. There is no end to the hiking, camping, fishing, sailing, surfing, snowboarding, skateboarding, and Rollerblading. Also, every nationality in the world is represented here, with all the cool food that goes along with that.

And where else could four little boys have the opportunity to see giant, sexually explicit billboards of some plastic human Barbie doll named Angelyne everywhere we drive? Or the billboards for Adam/Eve, the adult toy store? Or the one for the Spearmint Rhino, a "gentlemen's" club? And what would L.A. be without a drive-by shooting now and then?

Oh, well. Maybe in heaven. Maybe there we'll get to have the best of both worlds. The gentleness of Cleveland with the vitality of Los Angeles. A place where the kids play in the leaf pile all by themselves while the parents enjoy some Korean barbecue and hot sake.

Okay, so we may have to wait awhile until we get there. In the meantime, see you in the front yard.

MOM

THIS IS WHAT I REMEMBER ABOUT MY MOM:

She wasn't a girly-girl. She didn't wear makeup. She did wear white blouses and navy blue skirts and deck shoes. And little sweaters knit in that popcorn stitch. Maybe this was because she came from a family of fifteen kids and fashion was probably not high on the list of necessities.

· · ·

She got a doll only once in her life. It was Christmas, the doll's head was porcelain, and it was broken that same day. No re-placement. Again, the fifteen-kids thing—you pretty much got one shot at a toy.

· · ·

One morning—I was three or four—the mailman delivered a brown box along with the regular mail. I was stunned when my mother took the package, then turned to me and said, "Oh, this one's for you." I opened it to find a little tin tea set inside that my mom had ordered off the back of a cereal box. You would have thought she'd handed me the Hope diamond for the reaction it elicited from me. "Oh, Mom, thank you, I LOVE you!" It was my first experience of having another human being do a loving, kind, and unnecessary gesture simply because she loved me and because it gave her pleasure to give me pleasure.

. . .

She went to mass seven days a week.

. . .

In the second grade, my mom sent me to a Halloween costume party on the wrong day. I walked two blocks in a gypsy costume (an old Heidi dress with lots of plastic-bead necklaces and a bandana around my head), and when my friend answered the door, she told me that the party was yesterday but that they had saved my treat cup. I slunk back home with the paper cup of peanuts in my hand, feeling completely humiliated and vowing never to trust my mother again. Thirty-nine years later, I did the same thing to my kid.

. . .

The day my mom's dad died, she lay facedown on the couch in the living room and cried for a long time. I was pretty young, probably about four, and I kept asking her why she was sad. She just kept on crying and didn't answer me. My dad finally told me to leave her alone.

. . .

She showed me how to chop walnuts for brownies, make meatballs, polish silver, and vacuum.

. . .

Money was a bit tight in our family, but my mom always signed me up for extracurricular activities. I went to an art class, one year of ballet, and one summer of drama. I was also the only one to get braces, albeit on discount because we really couldn't afford the whole shebang so she found a dentist who was almost an orthodontist but needed some practice. Something about me must have made her think she should start grooming me for a life in the performing arts—probably the fact that I was a huge showoff, always singing, and constantly forcing my neighborhood friends to act out whatever book I happened to be reading.

. . .

Once, in the first grade, I failed a math test, and I had this really bad, crappy feeling inside the whole way home. When I walked into the house and saw my mom, I burst into tears and told her what happened, afraid that she might yell at me. She just scooped me up in her arms and said, "Don't worry about it," and held me until I stopped crying.

. . .

She really liked Motown, especially Smokey Robinson.

. . .

My mom was a very good tennis player. One of my favorite activities in the summer was being the ball girl during her matches, especially when she was playing with my cute boy cousins. I only recently received an old newspaper clipping from my friend Joe Maxse, the boxing writer for the Cleveland *Plain Dealer*. He ran across it while looking up some old fight info. It said my mom won the city women's tennis championship, defeating a woman named Babe Dallas. That's my mom: the woman who beat Babe Dallas.

. . .

She used to be an ice-skater too, and rumor had it that she won some speed-skating competitions when she was a girl. I never saw her on the ice, but she kept her old brown skates on a shelf in the basement, and they fascinated me. I used to go down there and just hold them, look at them, imagining my mom as a champion, having a life outside our house, our family, outside of me.

. . .

One night after dinner, when we were all reading or doing our homework, Mom surprised us by coming downstairs in a new black chiffon dress. It had long, puffy, see-through sleeves that gathered at the wrist in red and yellow shearing, with the same shearing at the waist and at the neck. She asked us what we thought of it. I was particularly enthusiastic about it, because until then she was still wearing rather dowdy and threadbare shifts from the sixties. We all agreed we loved it. She took it back to the store the next day.

. . .

Every day when I came home from school, I would find my mom in the basement, ironing. Every day.

. . .

The girls in our neighborhood made a nasty habit of leaving one or the other friend out of the loop on a daily basis, and one particular day Sally Greene and I told Suzie Albertz with the long hair that we wanted to play alone. Well, it didn't take long for the neighborhood drums to beat, and my mom showed up at Sally's door, telling me never to treat anyone like that again. My mom was fairly quiet, so when she spoke it had some weight behind it. At those times I always felt like a creep exposed. And it felt worse that my mother saw me that way. I would rather have been spanked.

. . .

I remember my mom yelling only once. She used to stack our clothes and books on the stairs, assuming we would pick them up and take them to our rooms on our way up. One day when all five of us were busily ignoring the stacks on the stairs, she exploded big-time. "YOU KIDS NEVER EVER HELP ME AROUND HERE. ALL I EVER DO IS PICK UP YOUR STUFF, SO *PICK UP YOUR STUFF*!!!!" So we did. At least *that* day.

. . .

My mom always made me get pixie haircuts, which were easier for her to take care of. It was such a short, choppy cut that when all was said and done I looked like I'd just been prepped for a lobotomy. Mom would take me to the local beauty parlor, a place done all in pale pink with those big hair dryers that looked like they came out of a bad science fiction movie. All the dear old blue-hairs would ooh and aah and mutter "So cute" as I walked by. No matter—I still hated it, and even more so because the old gals loved it. And then Twiggy came along and gave pixie haircuts a good name. Forever after I told my mom I wanted a Twiggy cut. She obliged.

. . .

Mom tried to get me to stop wetting the bed by giving me gifts. Once or twice a week I was promised a prize on my dresser in the morning if I didn't wet the bed. Mom had been spending many months coming into my room at midnight, waking me, sleepwalking me to the toilet, making sure I didn't throw the toilet paper down the laundry chute, helping me pull my pants back up, and sleepwalking me back to bed. She thought prizes might help. They didn't. I'd wet the bed, and still find some little thing—a statue of the Blessed Virgin with blue rhinestones in her halo, a poodle made out of hangers and yarn, a deck of cards. She continued the midnight run for another two years.

. . .

When César Chávez came on the political scene in the sixties, Mom made a point of not buying grapes in solidarity with the migrant workers. I thought that was pretty cool. My mom, the rebel.

. . .

Mom showed us how to make Boston coolers with vanilla ice cream and root beer, and it became part of a Friday night ritual that included watching *Johnny Quest* and looking through our photo box. The photo box was an old hatbox that contained hundreds of old family photos of my mom and her fourteen brothers and sisters. I loved seeing her in sepia tones wearing high button shoes, looking like she just stepped out of an "Our Gang" movie.

. . .

The hardest thing to handle was when my mom got her substitute-teaching license and started showing up at my class to fill in. She had terrible handwriting, and when she tried to do the penmanship lesson I could hear the kids snicker. I nearly willed myself invisible.

. . .

Mom took us for a new Easter outfit, including hat and shoes, every year. This was probably to make up for the one hour on Good Friday (between three and four o'clock) that we were made to sit in a chair and contemplate Christ dying on the cross. To this day I feel guilty and sort of naked before the eyes of God if I'm out and about between three and four on Good Friday. Talk about reach.

. . .

One night at dinner, Mom handed out blue sheets of paper with a new before-meal prayer on it, and had us read it every night until it was memorized. And we didn't substitute it for the old one—we added it onto what we already said, thereby creating a world's record for the longest grace in history: "InthenameoftheFatherandtheSonandtheHolySpirit.Amen.BlessusohLordandthesethygiftswhichweareabouttoreceivefromthybountythroughChristourLord.Amen.DearSacredHeartofJesusrememberthatweareconsecratedandbelongtoyou.Blessandprotectusall.Makeourhomeashrineofyourloveandyourgrace.Strengthenthebondofaffectionthatunitesustogether.Helpustobearoneanother'sburdensinpeaceandharmonyandunselfishness.KeepusalwaysclosetoyouandtoyourBlessedMother.Amen.MaythesoulsofthefaithfullydepartedthroughthemercyofGodrestinpeace.Amen.InthenameoftheFatherandtheSonandtheHolySpirit.Amen."

The one benefit to this exercise was that when there was company for dinner, we couldn't wait to see how many times they crossed themselves in the middle of the prayer, thinking it was over, and then be uncertain whether it was safe to pick up their forks, for fear of another prayer starting.

. . .

I remember Mom saying *shit* one time and one time only. She was vacuuming the living room and knocked over a potted plant, spilling dirt on the carpet. I was mortified.

. . .

Mom watched *The French Chef,* with Julia Child, religiously each week on PBS, taking copious notes on a stenographer's pad about things like beef Wellington. Oddly, we never saw anything that slightly resembled a Cordon Bleu creation. What we got were the same seven meals each week: meat loaf, spaghetti and meatballs, burgers, pork chops, chicken, and fishsticks. I had never thought of my mother as a great cook until I had kids of my own. Now every night I pray the little monsters don't write a book in which *my* cooking skills are evaluated—My *Life in the Stouffer's-Macaroni-and-Cheese-Please Cult.*

. . .

I remember Mom and Dad fighting only one time, but it was a doozy. My oldest sister, Sharon, wanted to wear fishnet stockings, and Dad would have none of it. We were all sitting at the dinner table, and Mom was quietly defending Sharon, when Dad threw down his napkin, saying he'd had it, and stormed out of the room. We all sat there, silently weirded out, and a few years down the road Sharon not only eschewed fishnets but became a nun. Hmmm.

. . .

That's about it. You'd think I'd remember more, but that's the thing about moms. When you're a kid, a mom is sort of like air, always there, inside you and outside you, keeping you alive, and yet you're barely aware of it. What she does for you doesn't really hit home until you have kids of your own. And suddenly, you get it. And hopefully, you forgive her any mistakes she made and thank her for everything else.

Thank *her*. What am I saying?

Thank me. Or else you're grounded.

FAIR TO MIDLAND

I RECENTLY READ that there was a vote in some school district to ban the game dodgeball from phys-ed classes and recess. For you less fortunate folks who don't know what I'm talking about, dodgeball is one of the all-time great elementary school games. This is how it goes: the phys-ed teacher, Miss Manley, leads the class to the cafegymatorium, divides it in two, hands each team about twelve big red rubber balls, then proceeds to let everyone try to blast the crap out of the other team. If you get hit, you're out. Last one standing wins. Genius in its simplicity, plus it saves Miss Manley from having to think up a lesson plan for that day.

Apparently, the rather aggressive nature of the game does not sit well with today's Barney generation. It was okay when *Tom and Jerry* was the standard, but not highly regarded since Raffi came on the scene singing about baby belugas (good-bye, caviar!). For cryin' out loud, what's a kid supposed to do with all that energy? If you let kids play dodgeball every day, they'd be so tuckered out you could take half of them off the Ritalin!

Somehow we've gotten to the point where we're not allowed to express any kind of anger or aggression, unless of course someone lights up a cigarette within fifty feet of our personal space. So what's a kid supposed to do with all that stuff? I'll tell you what *we* used to do . . .

In quaint, beautiful Bay Village, where I grew up, I had a gaggle of girlfriends all around my age who I still keep in touch with; we're all moms, we all go to church, we volunteer for all the school stuff, and yet. . . our childhoods were anything but genteel.

When I was growing up, one of our favorite games to play was Nazis. We were an angelic group of six-, seven-, and eight-year-olds, all with pixie haircuts (the hairstyle known as Mom's best friend), except for Suzie Albertz, whose mom let her hair grow long, which made us all jealous. (She also was the only one with a canopy bed—damn.) Picture us running around the neighborhood screaming "The Nazis are coming with guns and pitchforks!" The pitchforks were used to impale our babies.

That's right. We made high drama as we cried and begged for them not to kill our children, fell on the ground weeping as they impaled them, tried to comfort one another, and finally somehow found our own weapons—guns and pitchforks—and returned the favor. I'm talking about *girls* now, you understand. This was long before Sam Peckinpah and *Straw Dogs*, or Quentin Tarantino and *Reservoir Dogs*. We were Nazi Killer Dogs. We weren't even Jewish and we *loved* that game.

Then there was a weird scenario we used to perform called

Brave Tomboy. One of the older girls in the neighborhood, Sue Lily, who normally wouldn't spit on us if our hair was on fire, was apparently bored one day and decided to teach us what became our favorite game. Maybe it was our favorite because Sue Lily was too cool to play with us because she was thirteen, but for a few magic moments she deigned to talk to us and toss us this crumb. It was like a movie pitch.

We all lived in an orphanage (Jenny Sour's garage), run by a horrible couple who beat and starved all of us. This is what a quaint, beautiful, and safe environment does to the imagination of seven-year-old girls.

One night, Brave Tomboy comes knocking on the orphanage (garage) window, and helps us plan an escape for the next night. Now, the one strange thing about this is that Brave Tomboy was actually a boy. I mean, I *think* he was because someone always had to fall in love with him. We were either confused or latently gay. Or *overtly* gay.

Anyway, we escape out the window (which we really did—it was low to the ground—the best part of the game) and run for our lives as the mean couple chases us with—you guessed it—pitchforks. Brave Tomboy leads the way down to the ship (Jenny Sour's picnic table), and we set sail just as the mean couple reaches the dock, where they fall in and drown. Yeah!

Since the picnic table was situated right under a tree, we had a built-in mast, which was cool and scary to climb. Someone played the part of Brave Tomboy's lover, and the two of them would sit on the upper deck while the rest of the orphan children slept below. Just as Brave Tomboy is about to plant one on the lover (no one in this game had actual names, only working titles), pirates suddenly appear on board and attack us with swords and . . . pitchforks.

So all the orphans below wake up and battle and kill the pirates. Since there were only five of us playing this game, we each had to play an orphan *and* a pirate at this stage, so we ran around the yard screaming at ourselves and stabbing ourselves and then we'd fall down dead (pirate) and get up again (triumphant orphan). And then we'd sail off. And that was the end of the game. Then we would start over so everyone would get a turn to play all the parts.

Now, it wasn't all violent, nightmarish games. We had a club (in Sally Greene's crawl space), which consisted of a president (me or Sally), a vice president (Jenny Sour), a secretary (Suzie Albertz with the long hair), and, since we ran out of titles, a janitor (Amy Greene, the youngest and therefore incapable of protesting to any effect, though she tried anyway). And then my little sister, Franny, who was so young she just kind of tagged around like a mascot. We traded titles at each meeting so we could take turns being president, except for Amy, who always had to be the janitor. We actually tried to force her to clean up the room after our meetings, which she would not do, even after we threatened to remove her title. Ingrate.

The club's sole purpose was to collect dues, so we could then spend them on stuff at the five-and-dime. We collected enough to buy rabbit's-foot key chains, which then became the secret symbol of our club.

As a club we would regularly take bag lunches and hike in the nearby Normandy School woods. We would "build" forts—

take a few sticks and lay them in a square, then sit in them and eat our picnic. Until we got bored, when we would then imagine big scary men crashing through the trees with knives and you-know-what and we'd all run screaming. Once we decided to make a club "time capsule" by taking a jar and filling it with treasure—a penny, a pencil, a note from all of us with the date on it—and burying it to be found a hundred years later. From what I've read about the exciting items buried in other time capsules that have been dug up lately, we weren't far off the target.

And as a foreshadowing of my future career, we all learned the song "America" from *West Side Story* and performed it on roller skates on the loading dock in the back of Heinen's, the local supermarket. Actually, there were many musical performances. After seeing *Mary Poppins* three times, we would go to the playground at the public school, get on the swings, and sing every song at the top of our lungs. *Twice*.

It all sounds idyllic, and it was. But human nature always reared its ugly head, and it was usually between me and Sally. We used to battle for the position of neighborhood *grand fromage*. We were both extremely opinionated and always wanted our way, and more than once we ended an afternoon by standing in someone's driveway yelling, "You think you're the big QUEEN!" "No, *YOU* do!" "NO, YOU!" "QUEEN!" "QUEEN!" Needless to say, we are still best friends.

Maybe it's because her house was always the most fun. They had five kids, like us, although they weren't Catholic. Five was just the norm in those days. They never locked their doors, and in the later teenage years, if I got home after my dad locked up, I could always stroll into the Greenes' house at midnight and crash on one of their extra beds. There were a couple of mornings when I woke up to Mrs. Greene's voice calling up the stairs, "Patty, are you up there?" And then saying into the phone, "Yeah, she's here."

And the Greenes were always willing to try something new. While I come from a long line of worriers (on my dad's side), the Greenes never gave a second thought to hiring a pony for a birthday party, or bringing home total strangers for an extended stay. One year it was the Brits they met on their Canadian vacation, named John and Sonia Baldry. They used words like *petrol, motorcar,* and once even slipped with *bloody,* which was the subject of curious conversation among us kids for some time.

The introduction of their culture into my young life might well be responsible for my choice of a British husband. (Can you sue a person for something like that?)

And one summer they went to a church supper and came back with four Italian studs who rocked the neighborhood. Apparently, Marco, Marco, Marco, and Beppi (they sounded like a Marx Brothers law firm) were traveling across the United States and stopped at the church for a free supper. Dick and Maryjo Greene invited them to stay, and we girls swooned around them for the next week. Like true Italians they tried to hit on all of us, and it was weird and scary and thrilling.

The other thing about the Greenes was that they were just plain fun. Mr. Greene used to walk us all to the Dairy Queen on summer nights, and we watched thunderstorms from their big front porch. When they got a dog, Dick walked him door-to-door up and down the street, the gaggle of kids growing larger with each stop, asking neighbors to vote on a name. ("Gunther" won. As in Gunther Tootie on *Car 54, Where Are You?*)

And once, when Mrs. Greene decided she wanted a different color carpet in the bedroom, she bought seventeen boxes of blue Rit dye and got all of us girls to grab sponges and help her. We spent hours dipping those sponges in bowls of dye and rubbing that carpet from wall to wall. We spent the whole summer sporting blue hands. And feet. The dye tended to rub off when you walked on the carpet. Which can be kind of inconvenient, since that's what carpets are for—walking on.

But Mrs. Greene's creativity rubbed off on us (no pun intended) in other ways. We were the most imaginative and entrepreneurial group I know. We gathered up old bedsheets and made American Indian dresses, wrote and performed plays, had summer fairs and bake sales.

And Suzie Albertz's mom had a creative side to her too. Martha Stewart had nothing on Camille. It was at her house that I learned to make Ukrainian eggs—the ones where you use a small wax melting tool to drip on designs between layers of dye, a painstaking process that only a dedicated (or bored) mom could watch kids do for hours. And she was the only person who actually had a taffy pull in her kitchen—never mind the mess. She was also the only mom who served tomato juice as the dinner beverage instead of milk, and made you drink the whole thing or you couldn't leave the table, even if you were a neighbor and, as such, a guest, and shouldn't be made to sit there for an hour after everyone else had gotten up.

And even though she whupped me on the butt with a belt once for jumping on the beds (her kids got more), she never raised an eyebrow the night I slept over on their new chaise lounge and wet it straight through. Plus they always had bags of red hots and chocolate chips, and kept boxes of baby zwieback teething toasts to chew on just 'cause they liked the taste. Some fun!

—

IT WAS ALL so much fun back then. It was a different time and the world was a different place. Our parents would let us run the neighborhood wild between meals. In the summer the only rule was to be home when the streetlights came on. The neighborhood was communal. So maybe we were a bit more aggressive, didn't have sensitivity training, got whupped by other people's moms. But it was a blast, and I'm sorry I can't give the same thing to my kids as long as we live here in L.A.

Writing down these memories has me thinking about Sally, Suzie, Jenny, Amy, my sister Franny, and the rest of the gang back on Midland Road. I want to send them something special to commemorate that magic time in our lives.

I was thinking maybe pitchforks . . .

NEW YORK CITY

CARMIE

THE DAY I FOUND OUT the cast of *Raymond* was going to Italy to shoot the season premiere was memorable not only for the thrill and joy of that news but for something else too. As I walked out of the meeting where the trip was announced, the first person I saw was Carmen. Carmen Vargas. Good ol' Carmie. One of our production assistants. "Did you hear about Italy?" I asked her. "Yeah, I'm going too! Phil [our producer] asked me to come with him and the family to help out as a nanny. I've already signed up for Italian lessons!" We smiled at each other and said almost at the same moment, "Can you believe it?"

We were both thinking the same thing: who would have ever guessed fifteen years ago that the two of us would be here now working on a hit television show, and shooting the opening episode of the fifth season in Italy?

Not us, that's for sure.

See, Carmen Vargas and I go back a ways.

It was 1987. I had been in Manhattan for seven years at that point and had experienced my share of ups and downs. The fact was the downs were dominating that contest. My acting "career," with the exception of a few highlights, had been spotty at best. I had a brief, ill-considered marriage behind me, and at the age of twenty-eight I was still scrambling to make ends meet like a college student, doing several part-time jobs, knowing that just about every girlfriend from high school and college was married, had kids, had homes, had real jobs.

And me? I was a copy clerk at *People* magazine two days a week. I was a proofreader in mergers and acquisitions at Morgan Stanley from midnight to eight A.M. I waited tables at various establishments, shoe-modeled when possible, and in between I auditioned for every ding-dong thing you can imagine: movies, plays, commercials, and industrial shows. I was doing everything except impersonating Cruella de Vil at kids' birthday parties. Mostly I impersonated her on dates.

It wasn't like I hadn't had *any* success. Okay, actually I'd had no success. But I seemed to have had just enough encouragement to keep me hanging on. Mere toeholds on the side of Mount Showbiz. At that point I only felt comfortable hoping to one day have more closet space; certainly I didn't dare entertain the idea of actually "making it."

Making it would have included being able to pay rent without giving blood, or not needing three roommates to pay the rent in a two-bedroom apartment, or not skipping regular meals. Making it would have included actually having an agent, getting auditions, and (heaven forfend!) getting a job that lasted longer than a day.

Perhaps I exaggerate. I had done a Pabst Blue Ribbon beer commercial (with Jason Alexander!), the residuals of which helped pay some bills. I got a chorus role in a short-lived Broadway gospel show called *Don't Get God Started*. And I once interviewed with Dustin Hoffman. At seven A.M. In my room-service-waitress uniform. As I poured him coffee in his hotel room. He was very kind and took pity on me in my faux French polyester costume with the cheesy ruffles at the neck and cuffs. He gave me his card. I gave him my head shot and résumé. I never heard from him again.

I was pretty familiar with rejection at that point. They say you need leather balls to play rugby. Rugby's for babies. Auditioning for acting jobs is tough. Instead of physical lumps and bruises you get emotional ones. Your knees aren't the first to go, as in rugby. In most cases it's your confidence. Then you turn into one of those ladies walking down Eighth Avenue pushing a stolen shopping cart full of empty pop cans, wearing one slipper and a torn orange housedress exposing a dirty old bra, singing the theme song from *Fame*.

You need to be tough in this business. Or naïve. I was both. Growing up Irish Catholic in Cleveland helped. It left me feeling both the need to prove something and sure that anyone with an ounce of intelligence would recognize my brilliance the minute they met me. Having survived the seventh grade with braces and a bad shag haircut prepared me for the worst New York could offer. But there was a cumulative effect. After eight years of banging my head against eight different sublet walls, I was emotionally battered. Not getting acting jobs was a clear and present sign of failure in the material world.

Time was the killer. When I first moved to New York at the age of twenty-two every baby step seemed not only like a huge victory but also like a big adventure. It was all fun, fun, fun back then. The successful acquisition of a slice and an egg cream made me feel like Donald Trump. My older brother, Michael, had moved to New York a couple of years before I did. He was the struggling writer; I was the struggling actress; our friends were the struggling artists, painters, poets, playwrights, and dancers.

Manhattan was life on another planet. An extremely cool one. No more sorority meetings in oxford shirts and khaki pants planning some doofy float for Greek Week. This was the Big Apple! The Greeks ran all the coffee shops here. Or owned shipping lines. In New York you could be anyone you wanted to be, or as many anyones as you wanted to be, and nobody cared. In fact, I had a different set of friends for every persona I could come up with. And I felt creative. There was always something around to inspire me. Plays, poetry readings, cabaret shows, art openings (free booze!), downtown clubs, uptown restaurants. One month into my arrival my newly acquired studio-musician friend introduced me to my first taste of sushi. I learned what an empanada was (had to—I was selling them), found out how delicious Brie could be. And the potential for breakout success seemed to radiate up out of the sidewalk through my shoes. Everything was possible; there was nothing to fear. I didn't think twice about walking home more than a bit tipsy through Central Park at four in the morning. Untouchable. Even when I was attacked in the Columbus Circle subway station, I was just pissed off that the jerk had left a dirty footprint in the middle of my new white dress when he kicked me backward down the stairs. Adventureland!

When the money got low, Michael and I could always front each other some cash, and when we were emotionally low, we could always front each other a drink (or quaff it down for free after-hours at whatever restaurant I happened to be working). We wrote songs, drank sake, stayed out all night. It was a time of heightened awareness and the city provided an electric sense of self-drama. Which helped mask the fact that I wasn't getting work in any *real* dramas.

In 1984 my brother left New York for a newspaper job in San Francisco. I had one less friend and fan in Gotham. There were more triumphs and tragedies during the next three years, but I was becoming increasingly less optimistic about my career of choice. The polish was off the Big Apple. What was once an exciting bohemian lifestyle became a grinding hand-to-mouth existence. The sights and sounds of big-city life were becoming ever more ugly, harsh, and depressing. The place didn't smell all that great either.

There is no place more exhilarating when you're on top of the world than New York City. There's also no place more depressing when you're down-and-out. The sorry state of my existence was confirmed for me when my dear college roommate Kelly visited me in my studio sublet in the Village. She was charmed by my setup, but the report I heard after she went back to Ohio was "My God! Patty lives in a *closet!*" So there was a constellation of factors involved in my outlook, moving my daily mood slowly but steadily from blue to black. It was a progressive and scary feeling. That's when I remembered something my mother had always told me: when times get tough and you're feeling sorry for yourself, do something good for someone less fortunate. It will help that person, help you take your mind off your own troubles, and maybe give you some appreciation for the good things you *do* have.

My dear mom.

So I decided to enroll in a sign-language class. That would be the ticket! Not only could I be a saintly signer for the less fortunate, I might also be able to finally get a job in the theater, even if it was theater for the deaf, since no one else would have me. I think I made it through two lessons. God saw through my false altruism to the barely concealed self-serving master plan and promptly made sure it rained cats and dogs every time there was a signing class. Noah I was not.

Not one to let God think He was better than me, I tried again. This time I looked up a local chapter of Catholic Big Sisters in Manhattan and applied to be one. At this time in my life, I liked to blame all my problems on the fact that my mother had died when I was twelve, so I thought I would hook up with another dead-mother victim just to confirm my suspicions. And I thought that maybe I could show someone else who was motherless that she could have that awful experience and *still* end up as a depressed out-of-work actress. Or maybe I could just be a friend to her. I felt a little unworthy offering my services. I didn't have much in the way of money or entrée into any world other than my own. Which wasn't all that fabulous.

The woman at the agency told me that they had a girl who was difficult to place because she was older than the average little sister and was interested in becoming an actress. Carmen

Vargas, from Spanish Harlem, was sixteen years old. In one year she would be too old for the organization. Many people participating in the Big Sister program were looking for younger girls with whom they'd have a greater opportunity to develop a long-term relationship.

With my limited resources I thought Carmen and I might be a perfect fit. For all I knew, in a year I might be back in Cleveland looking for work. Maybe we could go there together and look for work. With Carmen being sixteen, we were a lot closer to being actual sisters than we were to having a parent-child relationship.

Since I didn't have much money for our first outing, which was also Carmen's birthday, I took her to see the Broadway show *Sarafina!* But all I could afford were those tickets where you stand in the back of the theater. Our feet were beat, but the show was fantastic. Afterward we went over to Ninth Avenue for something to eat at the Film Center Café, one of the coolest places around. There was almost no one in the joint, except for, of course, SANDRA BERNHARD and MADONNA! There is a God! Carmen and I were so excited, we giggled and stared and never worked up the nerve to say hello.

Since I was horribly broke all the time, our relationship became not so much about "doing things" but more about being together. She'd come over to my apartment and do her homework. We'd talk on the phone. She borrowed one of my audition outfits for her school dance. (Since I rarely had auditions, it was just about brand-new. Still had the tags on it, I believe.) On one of the rare occasions when I did have an audition, I needed some Spanish phrases for the character, so I called Carmie. She gave me some great stuff and I gave one of the best auditions of my life. The director actually thought that "Heaton" was an odd name for a Spanish woman. Still didn't get the job. I of course proffered much boyfriend advice to Carmen, always being much stricter with her than I was with myself. She saw right through it, but still listened a little bit. I went to her school play, went uptown to Spanish Harlem to see where she lived and meet her dad and her half brother and sister.

Shortly after we got to know each other Carmen confided in me that she was having real problems at home with her stepmother. She said there were times when she felt like she had nowhere to turn. Things had gotten so bad, she said she thought she might kill herself or her stepmother. I told her how I at one time had wanted to kill myself, but fortunately my only means was a rusty old Bic disposable razor and I was afraid I would get blood poisoning. (Sometimes laughter is the best medicine.) In many ways it was more like a real relationship because it wasn't about all the great places I could take her or all the gifts I could give her. We got to be buds. Carmen was around through several of my boyfriends and my husband-to-be. In fact, I distinctly remember Carmie almost ruining things with Dave when she walked in on me bleaching in the bathroom and loudly exclaimed, "I didn't know you had a mustache!" I don't want to overromanticize or TV-movie-ize it. We were two people lost in New York who found each other. One from the Dominican Republic, the other from Cleveland, Ohio. And we helped each other in ways we never imagined, even though we didn't know we were doing it at the time.

Carmen and I kept in touch after that first Big Sister year ran out. But several years later I decided that if this acting thing was going to last for me I needed to take it out to the West Coast because New York just wasn't getting the job done. "If you can make it here," Frank sang. But I wasn't making it there. I needed to go west. The day I told Carmen I was leaving was tough. We were walking through Chinatown and I was trying to explain that I really needed to make this move. It wasn't happening for me in New York. I told her I'd keep in touch. But I could tell she wasn't buying that either. We were both crying. I don't know who was taking it harder.

But I did keep in touch. A little more than two years later I was married and had my first son. Carmen had dropped out of college and was in some dead-end job. I thought maybe a change of scenery would help her and I knew I could certainly use some assistance, so I offered her the chance to come to L.A. I'm sure it seemed exciting to her at first. But we had only one car and Carmie didn't have a California driver's license, so she was stuck. And little Sam was a bit colicky, and Mom and Dad were even crankier. Our house was tiny, and Carmen had to stay in the bedroom next to ours and listen to us not have sex. So after three months, Carmie had had just about enough of the L.A. experience. After no success in applying to colleges in the area, she decided to go back to New York.

Flash forward: 1995. I'd been on three canceled television shows since Carmen was last out here. It was the first season of

Raymond. Ray had moved to California on the long shot that the show would get renewed. His wife, Anna, and three kids were still back in Queens waiting to see what would happen. On the set one day he mentioned how swamped his wife was alone back home with the three kids. They had the money for help but didn't know where to begin looking. By this time Carmen was living in her brother's basement in Queens and working at the Gap. She was thinking of moving in with her boyfriend, whom she wasn't that crazy about, but her brother needed his basement back. I had been harping on Carmen via phone not to move in with this guy—I told her that once she did it would be hard to extricate herself from the situation. When I heard about Ray's family's situation, I told him that Anna should call Carmen. She did. Not long after, Carmen was living with the Romanos as a full-time nanny. Not long after that, *Everybody Loves Raymond* was renewed for a second season. Ray moved the family out West. Carmen came with.

One thing led to another. Carmen looked after the kids. Carmen got a job as a production assistant on the set. Carmen got to know Phil Rosenthal, our producer, and started working over at his house, looking after his kids. When it was time to go to Italy, it was natural to have Carmen along.

And now I think back and remember that look we shared when we realized we were on our way to Rome, under the sparkling Mediterranean sun, while the breeze sailed over the ocean blue and everything seemed so meant to be. The way things work out sometimes makes you think. And marvel.

Life is never heaven on earth. But sometimes you get a little piece of it. Carmen and I knew each other when. And the friendship that grew from those rough-and-tumble times is special. Times have changed. We're both busy and don't often spend time together like we did. And things are *still* rough-and-tumble, somehow. But no less special. She's *still* my little sister Carmie, and now my friend.

Funny how that works.

Now, if she'd just quit borrowing my clothes.

SURVIVAL JOBS:
PART II

MY LAST JOB IN CLEVELAND, after I "graduated" from Ohio State (I use the term loosely—I stayed up all night on No-Doz to eke through my French final), really propelled me to New York. I had an offer from my friend KT to room with her in the Big Apple, but I wasn't quite sure, so I took a job at a restaurant in Cleveland called The Blue Fox. This place had a reputation for being a Mob hangout, and it had the waitresses to prove it. They all had names like "Dolly," "Lil," and "Bosoms" . . . I mean "Bunny" . . . and sported big, teased, dyed hair; red lipstick; low-cut, tight-fitting blouses; and short skirts. I showed up in a knee-length navy skirt and a blouse with a buttoned-up collar, my hair neatly coiffed in a bun, and comfortable shoes. I lasted about a week.

It was such a scary place, such a horrifying look into what could be my future, that I put in a 911 call to KT and said, "Give me twenty-four hours—I'll meet you on Fifty-fifth and Eighth." I got the cheapest flight I could find, packed up all my shoes, and took off with the eight hundred bucks my dad gave me to get started (he didn't like me working at The Blue Fox any more than I did).

I had given KT the go-ahead to just find a place, and when I arrived, I loved it on sight. A studio apartment conveniently situated above an empanada and ice cream store (only in New York) and right next door to The Possible Twenty, a studio musicians' bar. Within a week I was scooping ice cream at the store and drinking at the bar. I don't think it even had a name, because it served just about everything: meat pies, spinach pies, soup, ice cream, cookies, and jelly beans. It was the perfect little gig: I was never late for work, and KT and I could trade off if I had an audition (ha!). What a blast—the store was the size of a large closet, and I had the place all to myself. I'd turn up the transistor radio and sing at the top of my lungs; it was as if I were a mermaid singing a siren's song—young eligible guys would be lured to my lair, flirting their butts off with me. Not bad.

It turned out that the owner of the place, Judy, had another restaurant uptown called La Tablita (The Little Table). She and I hit it off, and soon I was managing there. I was a great hostess—cute and pleasingly plump with a wholesome midwestern quality, and able to remember names and table preferences. Plus, I got one free hot meal a day. Which was all I needed. The only difficulty I encountered was with a couple of waitresses there who hated my guts. They had been at La Tablita a little too long, and they hated Judy. As soon as they saw her treating me like her own daughter, I was dead meat. They barely spoke to me, and when they did, they were snotty and condescending. And when the restaurant got busy and I asked them to do something, one of them almost hit me. I encountered that occasionally. I was a hard worker, and I had that slightly annoying Ohio enthusiasm about me—a far cry from the cynical broad I am today. My optimism amused some, but rubbed others the wrong way.

But I had plenty of friends among the waitstaff too: Robert, the obligatory and hilarious gay waiter who nicknamed me "Twinks" (short for "Twinkie," as in Hostess Twinkie, which is what I was, the hostess); Anne, a modern dancer in one of the lower companies of the Martha Graham studio, whose shirts always smelled like Tiger Balm ointment and who took me seriously when I was depressed and told me to see a shrink; Doris, a Puerto Rican Marilyn Monroe who also worked out with me at Mid-City Women's Body Building—every male customer became paralyzed and drooled at the sight of her. At La Tablita I was introduced to skirt steak, flan, and chimichanga sauce. Magic.

La Tablita was the first of many restaurants I labored in. I had a short stint around the corner on Seventy-second and Columbus at a strange place called Mrs. J's Sacred Cow: it was a semiformal steak joint staffed with singing waiters. So not only did you have to keep dinner orders straight, it helped if you could belt out something from *Funny Girl*. There was a weird vibe among the staff: again, some of these people had tasted a bit of theatrical success in the third touring company of this or that musical, but now, consigned to singing for somebody else's supper, they made the most of it by lording their tenure over the newcomer (me). One gal prided herself on the fact that not only had she toured in some moth-bitten old production but she also claimed to have had an affair with Donald O'Connor, who was the star of it. Apparently he ended the whole thing (imagine being dumped by that corny old coot!), but she still carried the relationship around with her like some great honor and established herself as queen of the Sacred Cow. In other words, she was mean to me. I think I got up and sang one song, messed up somebody's order, and got the hell out of there. I mean, c'mon, if I'm gonna be forced to engage in backstage backstabbing, it had better be at a frickin' theater, not some two-bit steak house.

There was another short-lived singing-waitress job that ended before it started when the owner followed me up to the dressing room that had curtains that didn't close, watched me dress, then walked me to the door with his arm so far around me he could grab my right breast—and did. Still pisses me off when I think about it. My brother went over there and threatened the guy. I didn't go back to work there, and when he had the nerve to call and ask where I was, I told him I would call the cops if he bothered me again. He didn't call back. *Asshole*.

The best and worst time I ever had in a restaurant was a place called Downtown. It was run by this great young Jewish guy named Philip, and it was a blast. On my first day of work, I started getting menstrual cramps as I walked to the restaurant. By the time I reached the door, I could barely speak. I started sweating profusely, *this* close to passing out from the pain. (Other than chronic lateness, this was the other problem I had—debilitating periods. But no insurance equals no gynecologist equals no prescription painkiller.) God bless Philip, who didn't seemed phased at all as I hung on to the side of the bar. He found a waitress who did have insurance/gyno/painkillers, gave me two, and sent me to the basement, where I lay down and fell asleep on a table full of linens. Nice first impression.

But the next day was better, and pretty soon I was having a ball. The waiters were all great, especially Tim (who also called me Twinks) and Stephanie, one of the wildest girls I ever met and who ended up marrying Philip and settling down and having a family. Well, at least she had a family—I don't know if she ever settled down. There was a great Irish bartender there named Pascal, who was eventually fired for stealing; he was replaced by Dave, a big goofy former high school wrestler who didn't have a clue but was a really nice guy. And Jimmy. Let's not forget Jimmy, the busboy who saved my life.

Jimmy was a charming ne'er-do-well who tried to get away with doing as little as possible, but without a malicious bone in his body. He really stepped up to the plate the day I had the run-in with the biggest he-man woman-hater I had ever encountered—Cordell. Cordell was a big black short-order cook who hated women, especially white women, especially little white women from Ohio who were eternally optimistic and whose job it was to tell him what to do. Philip left me in charge of Sunday brunch one week, and for some reason, our usually quiet restaurant suddenly had a line out the door and a half-hour wait. We were packed and rapidly falling behind in our orders. I was frantically buying drinks for our customers, trying to appease them for the hour wait they were enduring for a plate of eggs. The waiters were complaining that the kitchen was out of control, their orders were coming in wrong or not at all, and Cordell was being uncooperative.

Well, I braced myself. I went into the kitchen and asked Cordell to please complete Lise's order; everyone at her table had been served except one person, and Cordell had moved that final order to the back of the line. Lise was in tears. I tried my best Norman Vincent Peale on him, saying I wasn't some uppity white woman trying to boss him around, merely an out-of-work actress trying to get through Sunday brunch. His reply? "I *hate* cookin' eggs." Oh. I thought it was me. Maybe he should have informed Philip of that *before* he took the brunch shift. Cordell threatened to leave. I screamed at him to get out. He did. And there I stood, alone in the kitchen, the Guatemalan food-prep guys staring at me blankly, wondering what to do next. And Jimmy. Jimmy, who was in the back rinsing the one dirty dish he been working on lovingly for twenty minutes. As I stood in the kitchen, fighting back tears, Jimmy said, "I'll do it. I'll cook." And he did. Just started banging out those orders like he'd been doing it all his life. God bless him, wherever he is.

Mostly the Downtown restaurant was fun. Too much fun. It had a great jukebox with Elvis Costello and the B-52's. Every night after work, a bunch of us would go out, after quaffing down four free drinks at the bar (sorry, Philip), and do the club scene till dawn, ending up at the Empire Diner at five A.M. having breakfast alongside transvestite prostitutes. Fabulous. But all the partying started to catch up with me, and I developed debilitating back pain, hives, and depression. So my good friend Philip fired me. That's right. He let me finish ringing out all the receipts, close out the register, then handed me an envelope and said, "That's all we're gonna need." Stone cold. For a minute I didn't get it, but when I saw the hundred-dollar bonus in the envelope, I realized he was paying me to go away. I guess my personal woes were bleeding too much into the job—the front of the house needs to be a bit more inviting than I was capable of.

I had never been fired before, and the humiliation of it was worse than not having a job. I was really angry at Philip, but more for the way that he fired me than for the firing itself. Ultimately he was right; I needed a change of scenery. My hives and back problems went away, and after a few weeks of walking around the streets of New York talking to myself ("WhatamIgonnadohowwillIpaymyrentIhavenoskillsI'm-doomed"), I landed a job as a room-service waitress at Le Parker Meridien. It's still there on Fifty-sixth and Sixth, a big French hotel with real uniforms and health insurance. Sounds like a big step up, right? Well, if you consider being the only woman on the six A.M. breakfast shift full of chauvinist pigs a step up, then yes. If you consider being greeted fifty times each morning by people in their underwear with morning breath a step up, then yes. There was a bit of glamour attached—I waited on the likes of John Denver (in his underwear), John Cougar Mellencamp (in his underwear), and Dustin Hoffman (fully dressed—God bless you, Dustin). I rode up in an elevator with Teri Garr, who was at the peak of her career after *Young Frankenstein* and *Tootsie*. Ten years later I was costarring

with her in the short-lived sitcom *Women of the House.* Ya
never know.

The only thing that made that job bearable was Michael
Cohen. Why are gay waiters so damn funny? Michael made
every day a pleasure, and in the mornings when I was flagging
down a cab at five-thirty A.M. to get to work, I knew that at
least I could look forward to a good laugh. We amused ourselves by speaking in French accents or pretending we spoke
no English at all, so that the hotel guests would have to gesticu-
late and speak loudly to make us understand what they wanted.
We played "Parisian espionage," and skulked around from floor
to floor, meeting on the stairwell, passing coded messages, and
smoking invisible Gauloises.

There was one magic moment with Michael Cohen that
captures his whole style. It was December, and one Sunday he
and I strolled down Fifth Avenue after work. It was very early,
and we had the whole street to ourselves. We were playing
"Macy's Thanksgiving Day Parade" as we walked: an imaginary
microphone in one hand, the other hand holding in our imaginary earpiece, commenting on all the sights as they went by.
Me: "I don't know about you, Bryant, but if I had to ride on
the Strawberry Shortcake float, I would have committed suicide by now." Michael: "You bet, Katie—I just saw one of the
Berry Best Friends take a flier back on Forty-sixth Street, and it
wasn't pretty." Suddenly Michael covered my eyes and said,
"Don't look!" He walked me another block and said, in his best
French accent, "A leetle Christmas geeft for you, mon petit
croissant!" He uncovered my eyes, shouted, "Surprise!" and

there before me was the Cartier Building, gift-wrapped in a gigantic red bow. It was something Cartier did every year, but *I* didn't know that.

I was living in Los Angeles when I heard that Michael had died. And you know, there wasn't a thing in that Cartier store that was more priceless than his humor and generous spirit.

—

NEW YORK IS FULL of many opportunities for advancement, and not just at restaurants. My dad was concerned about all this food-service business, and decided he'd take matters into his own hands and call in a favor from his old friend George Steinbrenner, another Cleveland native. Dad told George I was in New York, and asked was there anything he could do for me? Next thing I know I'm heading out to Yankee Stadium and meeting the big guy himself. I tell him I'm studying to be an actress, so he sets me up with James Nederlander, only the biggest producer on Broadway. A week later I'm having lunch at the Plaza with the two of them, totally unprepared for this, out of my league and neither of them knowing what to do with me. George even takes me to Elaine's, the favorite haunt of the glitterati. I'm inappropriately dressed in a cutoff sweatshirt and jeans (I've never heard of Elaine's), and when it comes time to order, I pronounce *scampi* as "scaahmpi" and am gently corrected by the rest of the table. *Cringe*.

George finally helps me secure a job as a copywriter for a party-planning company, which has nothing to do with acting, but at least he can tell my dad where I am Monday through Friday.

The gals at this company were great, and I still count them among my dearest friends. They knew I only got the gig because of George, but they took me under their wing anyway. The job consisted of setting up big charity events in New York and rubbing shoulders with all the swells—Donald and Ivana Trump, Frank Sinatra, Brooke Astor, Ella Fitzgerald. My immediate boss, Betsy Bromberg-O'Rourke, had gone to high school in Switzerland, then to the Sorbonne in Paris, and had a sweet little Upper East Side apartment where she introduced me to the finer things in life, like caviar and champagne. I was in awe of her and all her Euro-friends. I may as well have been Elly May Clampett, but Betsy was and is a terrific person who believed in me from the beginning. She always fed me and fixed me up with guys.

But I never lasted more than six months at most of these places; after a while, I had a hard time working up the enthusiasm to get up at seven A.M. for something I didn't really like doing. Now, I know some people spend all their lives getting up early to do work they don't enjoy, but that wasn't me—life is too short for that. Today my *kids* get me up at seven A.M. Now, life is too long. You can't win.

After a while at the party place I needed a new fix, so I called my brother, who was a copy clerk and freelance reporter at *People* magazine, and asked for an introduction. He came through, and thus began one of the greatest survival gigs anyone could ever have.

Now, some might not think that there is anything particularly special about running the Xerox machine at a magazine or taking dinner orders for a bunch of writers. My friends, I was in heaven. I worked only a few days a week, got free meals and health insurance, and hung around a bunch of nice, funny, intelligent people. My immediate boss, David Greisen, had been a good friend to my brother, and now was one to me. I had flexible hours, made free long-distance phone calls (sorry Time Warner—send me the bill), and attended the weekly "pours" that were held down the hall in the conference room. You see, this was the eighties, and money was flowing freely at every corporation in New York. Since this was a magazine, and a magazine has writers, and writers like to drink, someone always thought up an excuse to have a "pour," as in pouring champagne to celebrate whatever: Ted's promotion, Alice's new baby, Frank getting the spot out of his favorite tie.

Tuesday nights were the nights the magazine was put to bed (ready to print). It was normally a long night, deep into the A.M., and the company provided dinner at six, then again at midnight, when we would take orders from a local diner. Since we were in charge of the orders, my clerkmate Chico got the great idea of adding on his grocery list for the week. Along with the Reubens, grilled cheeses, and French fries were quarts of milk, eight jumbo Hershey bars, and tubs of butter. When Time merged with Warner Brothers, it all came to a grinding halt. But it was great while it lasted.

Everyone at *People* was very supportive too. I was producing and acting in a play at the time, and besides giving me the time off that I needed (thank you, David Greisen), all my coworkers, from the most senior editors to the lowliest copy clerks, came to see the show. It didn't hurt that I hung the rave reviews from *The New York Times* (with my mention highlighted) by the elevator. But it was just that kind of place. David Greisen gave me time off to go to Italy to model shoes, time off to do a Broadway show, time off to audition, and always held my job until I came back. (God bless you, David Greisen.)

The only catch was that I wasn't making quite enough money to survive, so when I wasn't playing at *People,* I was toiling as a proofreader across the street at Morgan Stanley in the mergers and acquisitions department. I had initially faked my way into the whole proofreading gig. Since I tested out of taking college English, I figured I was smart enough to proofread. I took an exam at a temp agency and passed, and I was on my way. Morgan Stanley, though a bit more impersonal, was a similarly cushy gig—decent pay, flexible hours, but slightly stranger people. The computer operators and proofreaders who worked the graveyard shift, midnight to eight A.M., were mostly people who couldn't get along with the kind of humanity that works during the day and sleeps at night. I also didn't get one date out of all the yuppies who worked there, probably because they were all ferociously committed to the acquisition of wealth, status, and power, as opposed to sensitivity, creativity, and charm. Or maybe I was just too fat.

But not too fat to model shoes! Yessir, four times a year I got to do the shoe show in New York, trying on different styles for buyers all around the country. The fashion retail industry is one weird snake pit, but it was only for a few days each year, I got a discount on the merchandise, and they paid my way to Italy one December.

You'd think that those would be enough jobs for anyone in

one lifetime. But I guess what all of this suffering speaks to is the magic, the calling, for me anyway, to be an actress. It must be special, otherwise no one would endure the trial by fire that is moving from the comfort of one's hometown to New York or Los Angeles and to suffer not only sure and constant rejection but all the restaurant jobs too.

I just say God bless every soul who walks this road. And I'm grateful I got the breaks that enabled me to wind up writing these words.

You know what would be a nice thing to do? Take an actor to lunch. You don't know any? They're waiting tables at a restaurant near you. You'll probably have to wait until they get off work.

If they're working a lunch shift, take them to dinner. If they're working dinner, take them to lunch. You know what? Forget all that. Just tip 20 percent. Actor or no actor.

It's a jungle out there.

MY FIRST LOVE:
NEW YORK CITY

THERE HAVE BEEN A LOT of after-the-fact love songs to New York City since 9/11. The on-line newspaper parody *The Onion* nailed it with the headline TEMPORARY NATIONAL OUT-POURING OF AFFECTION FOR NEW YORK CITY.

Funny.

Having grown up in Ohio but lived vicariously in New York through countless movies, magazine stories, and television news reports, you would think I might have arrived at least half-way experienced. But nothing could have prepared me for the sensory-overload experience of my first month in New York City in 1980. There was so much to see, hear, smell, taste, and feel. Not all of it was pleasant. But a lot was exquisite.

DINERS: Before Starbucks took over the world, there were and still are, I guess, corner diners where I would grab coffee before getting on the subway. The counter guy would see me coming and holler, "Cawfee regulah." A regular coffee in Ohio was black. In New York it means cream and sugar. I'd say, "No, I want cream and sugar." The guy would holler, "Cawfee regulah." I thought the guy was messing with me. Eventually he smiled and explained things. It was New York City's version of tough love. They have to mess with you a little to see what you're made of.

SUBWAYS: I used to love getting in the first subway car and standing and staring out the front window as the train flew down the track's dark hole. It was such a rush. I know, what a yokel. I'm not ashamed. Also, every single steel beam on the subway platforms back then had the graffiti "Jesus Loves You" on it. *Every single one.* Isn't that amazing? I used to try to find one that didn't have it. I never did. Who wrote all that? They were all in the same handwriting. And what would Jesus think of someone defacing public property in His name? This is the kind of deep thinking that living in New York inspires.

PIZZA BY THE SLICE: Genius. When I first moved to New York a slice cost $.75. In the earliest lean times I could feed myself for $1.50 a day. A slice at noon and another at nine P.M. Plus, you could doctor those babies with oregano, garlic powder, red pepper flakes. I learned how to fold the slice in my hand so that the cheese-grease ran off away from the crust and into the napkin. If I got work or was splurging, I'd get a slice with mushrooms, onions, and sausage. Oh, my God! And a chocolate egg cream for dessert. Which didn't contain eggs or cream. It was chocolate syrup, seltzer, and whole milk. Served in a paper cone in a stainless steel holder.

This was living.

CABS: At first the whole cab thing was like taking the space shuttle. And seemed as expensive. But there are no cabs in Cleveland. I mean, there *are* cabs. But they're only for going to and from the airport. That's it. But in New York, the idea that if you're late for something or you can't face the subway on one particular day you can grab a cab: how fun is that? Too, too fun.

NEW YORK STYLE: It's in the people's DNA. It's the most important city in the world and the folks there live up to that billing. It's not one look. But every look has its own remarkable signature. And there are hundreds. I was amazed to see homeless people who had put more thought into their looks than a lot of people in Ohio. No disrespect meant. Having and maintaining a look is something that's just there.

NEW YORK ENERGY: Everybody in Manhattan seems to be Major League. Even if they're Major League jerks. It's The Show. Nobody goes there to lie back. Everybody's chasing the dream. And it means something different to and for everyone. But it's a beautiful thing and it gives the city an adrenaline buzz.

Oh, and that thing about New York being the city that never sleeps: that's bull. It sleeps plenty. But when it's awake, watch out.

THE CIRCLE LINE: It's a double-decker tourist boat trip that circles Manhattan. On a nice summer day, riding on the upper deck with the wind in my hair and the sun on my face, looking at the skyline from the outside and trying to figure out how I was ever going to make it there: very therapeutic. It's nice to see the island from the *outside* every now and again. Also a *must* for killing an afternoon when your parents come to visit.

NEW YORK ANGER: I came from a home where expressing any kind of dissatisfaction in a loud or exuberant manner (or even in an under-your-breath mumble) was not the norm. It meant crisis. To see people yell and scream at each other all the time as a matter of course, or for no reason at all, was liberating for me. It was like: Let it out, you'll feel better. You've heard of road rage? This is rage rage. They don't mean anything by it. It's just their way, you *moron!*

SUNDAY BRUNCH: Again, pure genius. Any Sunday morning I could go almost anywhere for a $7.99 brunch that included a free Bloody Mary or mimosa—champagne and orange juice. Sometimes the second drink was half-price. So, it's been a rough week, you meet a bunch of friends after church, and you all get half a bag on, chat about your lives, go home, read the eight-and-a-half-pound *New York Times,* and take an amazingly deep and restful nap. Then you rouse yourself at four P.M., throw a load of laundry in, take a walk in the park, Central or Riverside, go home, watch television while finishing the *NYT,* and order Chinese takeout: hot-and-sour soup, fried pot stickers, and cold noodles in sesame sauce. Pure bliss. (If you have kids, you don't get to do any of this.)

NEW YORK DANGER: It's there. You have to be aware. You don't leave your doors or windows open when you're not there; you have to keep your wits about you at some level everywhere. It was not the crime-central city my father had warned me and worried about, but I had my apartment burgled, my purse grabbed, a gun pointed at my head, and a couple of other unsavory experiences that might have been avoided had I been better schooled.

But that *was* the school. Life in the big city in all its majesty and squalor. Like I said, New York attracts the best from every field, even, if not especially, criminal.

NEW YORK LOVE: For every act of cruelty and unkindness there were others of amazing unselfishness. New York wouldn't be the city it is today if the collective positive didn't outweigh the negative. I believe there is no better experience for a post-college kid than to spend some time striving for survival or even greatness in the Big Apple.

I'll always feel lucky that I lived in Manhattan during the eighties, which was not a particularly good decade for clothes, music, or hairstyles, but it was the last era in which Manhattan rents tolerated a middle class. And I lived all over that island in those ten years. I was the sublet queen.

Even though I wasn't born in Manhattan, or anywhere near it, and I don't live there now, I will forever consider it a home of sorts. I visit a couple of times a year. And it becomes more dear to my heart each time.

Of course I have a hell of a lot more money now.

Oh, yes, that's another thing about New York. If you have money, *everybody's* really nice and they let you do just about whatever you want.

And there's nothing wrong with that.

Personally, I recommend the Sunday brunch.

LOSING MY RELIGIONS

I WAS RAISED a staunch Catholic and now I am a staunch Presbyterian. And in between those two *staunches* was a very long road that I know has not ended. Most of that road was in New York. And quite a winding one it was.

It all started on the west side of Cleveland. When you grow up in an extremely devout Catholic family like mine, in a very Catholic city like Cleveland, the Holy Family and all the saints become permanent residents in your home and head.

We had statues of Mary and baby Jesus, the Infant of Prague in layers of silk and beaded gowns, which we treated like a Barbie doll. There were paintings of Jesus in the living room (never without the Sacred Heart in flames and encircled in a crown of thorns), rosaries, prayer books, scapulars, crucifixes, and well-worn paperback Graham Greene novels (*The End of the Affair*), all casually scattered about the house.

You'd never know what illustrated horrors awaited you when you thumbed through a volume of *Lives of the Saints*.

There were prayers when you got up, prayers before bed, prayers before dinner, and indecipherable prayers every Sunday at the Latin mass. Breathe in, breathe out—prayer was in the air.

There is beauty in the sense of security that such an upbringing gives a child. It also scares the crap out of you. Once, in the second grade, Sister Delrina said that for art class that day we could draw anything we wanted to. I drew a ragged picture of some poor naked, burning souls trying to get out of purgatory. The illustration included lots of flames and tortured bodies reaching up to heaven. Sister Delrina called my mom and asked where I had gotten that idea. Right out of an illustrated prayer book. My mom started putting them on the top shelf.

The notion of getting a black mark on your soul was also a big misbehavior deterrent. The idea that you carried around this soiled rag in your heart until you could get to a confessional to "launder" it would make any kid think twice. Especially if you were taught that if you died inconveniently *outside* the confessional box, the remaining black marks would be tallied up and determine how many years you would spend in the purifying fires of purgatory or, if they were bad enough, hell.

By the time I reached my sophomore year in high school, the burden became a bit too much to bear. Not only did I feel spiritually weighed down, but having gone exclusively to Catholic schools, I also felt culturally hemmed in. Everyone was Catholic, everything was Catholic, you dated Catholic, you married Catholic, you drank Catholic, you died Catholic. I changed to the local public high school.

It was nice to meet Protestants. They had fewer kids, their houses were nicer, they didn't wear uniforms, they didn't hang the bones of saints in a plastic bag around their necks. What a relief. And there seemed to be less alcohol involved. Lots of the kids I knew at Catholic school made a career of becoming raging alcoholics by the time they were eighteen.

At Ohio State I tried to make a fresh start with the One True Church, especially since the Newman Center was close to my dorm. There's a Newman Center on every campus; it's the Catholic student hangout, and for some reason the one at Ohio State seemed too liberal to me.

It was hard to have been brought up a hard-liner only to have the same church tell you a few years later that you could kinda ignore all the weird stuff that had been branded on your brain.

I wandered around campus for four years, bouncing back and forth between rowdy partying in a booze-fueled haze to handing out leaflets for Campus Crusade for Christ to unsuspecting students who just wanted to eat their Big Macs in peace. I couldn't graduate fast enough.

All the unresolved existential angst followed me to New York. But what a place to suffer! The first few months there I was having so much fun carousing that I didn't even call my brother, who lived only a few minutes away. But it takes only one or two cocaine hangovers to send you running back to church. (That's what happens when you move next door to a studio musicians' bar. The cocaine I mean, not the church.)

I met a bunch of Christian actors at an Episcopal church down in the Village. Grace Church had a long history in New

York, and a pretty hip congregation. A lot of young talented actors, artists, and musicians attended Grace, because the music was beautiful, the pastor was a woman, and it combined an ancient liturgy with modern sensibility. In other words, you could pretty much do what you wanted and still figure out a way to feel good about yourself.

Sort of. There is one thing that seems to characterize all the Christian artists whom I met. They were tortured souls. Every one of them, most of whom were and still are good friends, were always agonizing over the meaning of being out of work (what was God's plan for their lives?), sleeping with their girlfriend/boyfriend (was premarital sex really a sin?), portraying a prostitute (could one really glorify God that way?), and being a homosexual (don't even *try* to figure that one out).

Did the self-flagellation make anyone a better actor or writer or dancer? Not necessarily. I've found that God either gave you talent or he didn't, and no amount of praying can change that. Did the hair-shirt mentality make anyone a better person? Well, I can say from experience that it made the guys harder to date, and I wasn't any picnic either. I seemed to have no problem getting smashed on Saturday night, but at midnight (or six A.M.) I would excuse myself so that I could still make it to the eleven o'clock service on Sunday morning.

This went on with me no matter what church I went to. And I went to a lot of them. There was the one set up by a black Broadway musical star. Those services rocked. Almost the whole congregation was involved in musical theater, and the singing was better than the theater—and free. People would start improvising on the hymns, and it would turn into a Holy Spirit free-for-all.

The services were always pretty inspiring, but they also invited the odd insane person or two, who would start screaming some demonic-sounding gibberish at the top of their lungs, writhe on the floor, and have to be carried out. Newcomers were truly weirded out by that type of thing. We regulars thought nothing of it.

And then there was this one guy who showed up at every prayer meeting I went to, no matter what denomination it was. Apparently he had a direct line to God, because he always stood up in the middle of things and said he had a "word" from God. He proceeded to go on, speaking in first person as if God were channeling through him, e.g., "My people, you must heed my word!"

The first time I saw him I was impressed. And *de*pressed. Because obviously this guy was truly chosen, so in touch with the Spirit that he easily communed with the Almighty on a regular basis.

I, on the other hand, could barely get through an "Our Father" without my mind wandering off, thinking about my weight, or how I was gonna pay my phone bill, or wondering if I would ever get a legitimate acting job. After a while, though, I realized that this *was* this guy's acting job. He got his self-worth from being a self-appointed prophet. Finally, at the umpteenth prayer group around town, someone took him aside and gently suggested that he commune privately with God. Although one time he did call me at home (I used to give my phone number out to *anybody*!) and told me that God had given him a special word about me. God told this guy that I was going to be a very successful actress. Suddenly, he wasn't crazy at all, but obviously a clear-eyed visionary who knew God-given talent when he saw it, dammit.

That happened to me a couple of times, actually. The strangest people from all the many and various prayer groups I dropped in on over the years would be drawn to *me*. They would tell me that God was going to do something big in my life. And until the time when they said that to me, I had been thinking of them as total nutters. But once they prophesied my success, I knew that they were like the angel Clarence in *It's a Wonderful Life*—bumbling, but sent straight from the Almighty.

I finally found a Catholic church downtown that had a combination of tradition with some modern stuff. There was a small group of actors who were trying to bring drama and dance into the worship service.

This horrifying concept started around the 1970s, when the altar was hung with bad felt banners and we were forced to sing the now infamous "Kumbaya," complete with hand gestures. Bad ideas die hard, and here in New York at this little parish they were still trying to make mass "relevant." I ended up dancing around the altar in a leotard—me, with one year of ballet training in the second grade—waving a long piece of chiffon that symbolized who-knows-what, trying to illustrate some parable or something. I asked one male friend I had invited to the service what he thought, and he told me, "I've never seen so many bosoms on a Sunday morning." He had a point (but his pants covered it): here's a bunch of women in spandex hopping and leaping around the altar—it probably seemed more like a pagan fertilization ritual than Sunday school.

That was a fairly low point in my life. I was struggling with depression, and being out of work, or working at crap jobs, didn't help. And on top of that I had the added complication of trying to figure out what this all meant cosmically. Being bad didn't help my situation, but neither, it seemed, did being good.

I remember one particularly difficult day, when I decided that to pull myself up out of my rut I would serve the homeless at the soup kitchen after church. I would be able to lovingly serve hot meals to those who had less than I. All the while I would kindly ask after them, who they were, where they were from, and they would gratefully gaze up at me and bask in the warm light of my selflessness.

Needless to say, instead of serving, I was assigned to wiping down dirty trays, scraping bits of powdered mashed potatoes, salad, and bread crusts into the huge plastic garbage cans after everyone had left.

Enough. I'd had it. I politely but firmly told God that I was going to take a break from Him for a while. I had spent so many years bouncing around in a cosmic pinball game—trying to be good, trying not to sin, trying to keep that soul spotless, then bam! There I'd be, standing on the bar singing, "Momma's got a squeezebox," just before throwing up in the subway on the way home.

I tried to explain all this once to a priest in confession—I was weeping and telling him I was sick of myself and I didn't know what to do—and from behind the screen I could feel his disgust. He said I should just straighten up and then gave me a couple of rosaries to say as penance. Thanks for all the help and encouragement.

As I said, I decided to take a break from the whole God thing.

So, of course I immediately signed up for a New Age seminar. This was one that had been around for a long time, and for a mere five hundred bucks you could sit around all weekend with a bunch of confused losers like yourself and let a couple of jerks verbally beat up on you.

And it actually sort of worked. At least for a few weeks. Until the androids that worked at the seminar started hounding me to sign up for more courses, and refused to take no for an answer. I have never hung up on so many people in my life.

But there was a benefit to that weekend—it shook me up, and gave me the courage to start looking at the way I was seeing the world. I decided to explore a new worldview, and hightailed it to a therapist.

I feel for any parent whose child goes into therapy. Because about a month into the process, that parent is gonna get a call from their kid blaming them for just about everything the kid has ever experienced in life. So I would like to apologize to my dad right now for that call where I wept over the fact that one Saturday in the seventh grade he refused to be in the CYO basketball car pool.

So, that's the downside to therapy.

The upside is that for forty-five minutes a week you can tell all your deepest, darkest troubles to a professional listener, and if she's good, she never lets on that she thinks you really *are* crazy. She asks you a lot of questions in a calm, nonjudgmental manner, and little by little you are able to put the puzzle together, and see which pieces are missing.

Sometimes I didn't even say a word. One therapist I went to was a real earth mother—she wore big patchwork muumuus, her silver hair in a long braid down her back (think Colleen Dewhurst)—and all I did in her office for several sessions was weep. It was wonderful.

This worked for a while. But I often ran out of the funds to pay for it, and that would be about the time when I would conveniently find a new romantic interest to divert my attention.

I had a dear friend who started becoming as worried about my behavior as I was tired of it, and he dragged me to a new Presbyterian church. Thus began a phase in which I alienated just about everyone I'd ever met.

This little house church was run by a Jewish convert to Calvinism. Now, converts of any sort are always insufferably gung ho, and Calvin is the go-to guy if you're looking for the hard line. I called the pastor, weeping (as usual), and he told me to come on over to his house.

Well, he lived in Sheepshead Bay. So eight train transfers later I was sitting in his kitchen with him and his wife. After pouring my heart out to him, he said, "It would be great if you would go up to my study and maybe do some dusting there. I have so many books and it's hard for my wife to keep up with it." The request shocked me out of my depression.

I walked upstairs and started dusting, and immediately felt

better. One of their little daughters popped her head in later and said, "Are you still sad?" I said, "Not too," and I was hooked.

Maybe these folks realized I just needed some real family in New York, some routine, some security. Suddenly Sheepshead Bay was not too far to go, and I was hanging on every word the pastor said. I learned about Calvin and why he broke from the Catholic Church, and though it was scary, it made theological sense. In fact, it was a bit of a revelation.

Of course, when anyone has a revelation, he feels it his sworn duty to convince the rest of the world of the errors of their ways. I became quite impossible. There was no friend who was safe from my scrutiny of her every move, her every belief. I became self-righteous, arrogant, and *really* happy.

My brother, who had left New York for San Francisco and wound up writing a column back in Cleveland, came for a visit one weekend, all because I had told him what a great church I had found. I had The Answer. Now, my brother is about the kindest person you'll ever meet, and a devout Catholic. He's way into the Roman mystery and mysticism. Well, I couldn't wait to correct this last little flaw in him, and I knew he would be as blown away as I was at this new church. He was, but not in the way I expected.

He flew to New York to meet the pastor and they had what seemed to be a warm personal exchange of beliefs. A day later as we sat in the pew together, the pastor, from the pulpit, proceeded to rip Catholics to shreds, in the most mocking and condescending tone imaginable. I was horrified. My brother got up and walked out. I ran after him, and there proceeded

· · · 112 · · ·

the longest eight-train transfer back to the city. Fingers were pointed. Tears were shed. That pretty much cured me of that place.

To his credit, the pastor called me and wrote to my brother and apologized profusely. And, after all, the guy did save my life when he let me dust his study. We all fall short of the glory of God.

So, even though I'm not a hard-liner, I stuck with Presbyterianism. I bounced around a bit more in Los Angeles, waving my arms around here and saying a rosary there, but somehow now I'm just a white Anglo-Saxon Protestant.

What was the point of it all? Who was right in all of this? Let's just say that though the people I met and became friends with weren't perfect, their uppermost goal was to be good, kind, and thoughtful, and to try to walk through life with meaning and purpose; to put others before themselves and to act with integrity. They all seemed to have an awareness that God had reached out in love to them, and so, in kind, reached out to me, and tried to give of what they had and what they knew.

And when I hit those low points, I always remembered that the most honored saints—Abraham, David, Peter, Mary Magdalene, Paul, Augustine, Francis—all had some pretty questionable episodes in their lives, and yet God saw fit to use them for great good.

What they knew, and what I know, is that we're not perfect. Apparently God knows it too, or he wouldn't have bothered to show up here himself, and get strung up to straighten the whole mess out.

A priest once told me religion isn't God, and it isn't life either. Religion is a format, structure, or tool to remind us that God is *the* essential part of all good things. And life itself.

So much of the world is all about distracting us from the reality of God, our Father. The Great Spirit. He loves us. We need to love Him and each other.

Not our religions.

I've been a staunch Catholic and am now a staunch Presbyterian. I just want to be staunch in my love of God and everybody else.

I *try*, anyway.

He knows.

ROOM SERVICE FOR
THE SOUL

STRUGGLING AS AN ACTOR for so many years gave me a real yearning to taste the finer things in life. Like food and toilet paper. Although I never really wanted to *taste* the toilet paper. I would have settled for having it around when I needed it.

Back in my New York Holly Golightly phase (more like Holly Goes Nowhere at All—too broke) I would sit in my one-room apartment eating yogurt and Grape-Nuts for the third time that day and the third day that week, after washing my hair with a sample bottle of Pert I had grabbed from those kids handing them out on the street in midtown. I had rounded the block again and again for more samples, until I realized the kids didn't care and they just handed over the entire box so both they and I could go home. I remember shaving my legs with a six-month-old disposable razor, and I would crank up my "stereo" (a Walkman hooked up with two plastic minispeakers that I bought on Fourteenth Street for eight bucks) and fantasize about closet space, a manicure, a real meal.

It made me think about the story of the prodigal son who blew his inheritance on "riotous living" (I love that phrase). When he found himself a servant on a pig farm, he thought about the fact that the servants at his father's house were eating better than he was. There were a few occasions when I wondered what the family was having for dinner back in Cleveland. It wasn't Grape-Nuts. I knew that. The worst part: I wasn't even having a riot.

Now here I am "on location," being paid to make a movie and live in a beautiful hotel suite all to myself with room service, clean towels, and French-milled soap (as opposed to *Cleveland-milled* soap, I guess) fresh every day, and all the pillow chocolates I can handle.

And guess what? I miss my kids. I *long* for them. They've wrecked it for me, proving the famous saying "Your parents ruin the first half of your life, your kids ruin the second." Just when I start reaping the benefits of my position as TV mom and living a little, I can't stop missing them. Somehow, instead of enjoying my hard-won perks, I'm pining to have a little one crawl into my bed, lie on my head, then wet himself (and me) at six A.M.

It wasn't always this way. Hotel life was a longtime secret fantasy of mine. It started in 1966 when I was eight. My dad took the family on our annual summer vacation, this time to Washington, D.C. The seven of us drove eight hours straight in a canary-yellow Chevy Impala with no air-conditioning. In July. My dad had rented the car from a dealer he knew just for the trip. We were given strict instructions to keep the vehicle immaculate. I absentmindedly put a box of crayons on the rear-window ledge behind the backseat, and by the time we reached Wheeling, West Virginia, it had melted into a gooey, greasy Technicolor mess. (My dad went into anaphylactic shock the moment he saw the permanently stained backseat. It was a state of rage and disbelief so great it paralyzed him on the spot. We could have tied him to the roof of the car for the duration of the trip and he never would have known the difference.) But all was forgotten when we reached the hotel. And Dad reached the hotel bar. I'd never seen anything so glamorous in my nine years of life! It was the elegant Shoreham Hotel. My dad had been able to swing a sportswriter's discount rate. One of our rooms had a balcony! I felt like Cinderella.

And just to seal my fate, a movie called *The President's Analyst* was being filmed there. I stood on that balcony for hours watching James Coburn and Godfrey Cambridge film a car chase that ended with Coburn's Cadillac screeching right up to, but not going through, the hotel lobby. (Leonard Maltin gives the movie four stars!) James Coburn was the Hollywood movie star writ large in my memory. I ran up for an autograph after the scene. He was tall, tan, and handsome, and had a head full of silver hair, a mouth full of impossibly white teeth, and a booming voice of buttery oak. Couldn't have been sweeter. He looked and acted like he was enjoying life. So these were the kind of folks who stayed in hotels . . .

Just like the Heaton family. Fancy-schmancy! At least we felt that way. We had room service, ordered drinks and food by the pool, and basically swanned around. Jimmy Dean was performing there (pre-sausage), so was Spanish dancer Jose Greco.

We missed the Supremes by a week. There were giant posters of them in the lobby. One day by the pool Jimmy Dean asked my brother Michael to run and get him a Coke, then tipped him five dollars when he did! My brother was a little insuffer-able after his brush with fame. He still tells people he knew "James Dean."

But forget the pool—what put me over the edge was the hotel coffee shop. One morning, just Dad and I went down for some breakfast. How we ended up alone together was a mys-tery, but it added to the sacredness of the occasion. We sat at the counter (turquoise leather swivel chairs), and he said the magic words: "How about an English muffin?" I had never heard of such a thing. Dad ordered an English muffin and or-ange juice for each of us, and I felt like a queen. The muffin ar-rived with all those "nooks and crannies" filled with butter, and then I got to open those little square packets of jelly—what a treat! It was the most delicious thing I had ever tasted—and so exotic! Just me and Dad, sitting at the counter, munching our English muffins. I'm sure he doesn't remember it, but I think it's one of the only times we did something to-gether. I was hooked on hotel living from then on. Not to mention English muffins. My dad probably figures in there somewhere too. The big galoot.

That was probably the last time I hung out in a swank hotel until I moved to New York. And then I wasn't exactly hanging out in a swank hotel—I was working in one. Le Parker Meridien. Room-service waitress. Six A.M. Do you know what people look and smell like when they answer the door at that hour? Not pretty. I finally quit that job.

Where I was living was a 180-degree turn from suites in Le Parker Meridien. My apartment was in Hell's Kitchen. I shared it with my roommates Donna and Bob. You might know them better under their current names: Ma-Donna and Bob Redford. Okay, I made that part up. Never mind.

I read about the apartment in an ad in *The Village Voice*. It had everything I needed—midtown location and under $500 a month, plus two total strangers with whom I would have to share everything. I paid $450 a month for the privilege of sleeping on Donna's previous roommate's old futon (*eeeeewww!*). I never owned a stick of furniture in the eight years I lived in New York, because I was a chronic roving subletter. We all shared a tiny, cramped bathroom and a kitchenette that couldn't accommodate more than two people at a time, and even so, if you were standing on opposite sides you'd be rubbing butts. Which would be a good name for a rock band: the Rubbing Butts. Fortunately we all got along pretty well, even though Donna and I were grossed out by the fact that Bob made instant Potato Buds from a box every night for dinner, plus he would use up all my Pert shampoo.

Around this time I was working the graveyard shift at Morgan Stanley, proofreading in mergers and acquisitions. My job consisted of reading how corporate raiders were going to demolish some small company and ruin the lives of hundreds of families while a few CEOs would walk off with millions. I had to make sure they had spelled everything correctly ("Sir, I believe the word *annihilate* has two *n*'s"). I would wolf down some Szechuan chicken and cashews about three A.M. to get me through the shift, then drag my tired keister home at eight to try for a good morning's rest just as the construction crew outside our building started their pneumatic drills. A bit of a low point in my life.

And just then, my fairy godmother graced me with a job. I don't want to call it an acting job. It was more of a *performing* job. You know, singing and dancing. About shoes. Kinney shoes. That's right, singing and dancing about Kinney shoes. Sensible shoes. Quality at a fair price. It's what is known in this business as an industrial show. Not a lot of prestige, but usually good money and only one or two performances a week. And this industrial show would take me to Los Angeles, a place I had never been—I could only imagine the palm trees and limousines. In the past I had sent my head shots to various casting agents, telling them—*announcing*—that I would be arriving in town soon and I might be able to squeeze them in for an interview *if* they left a message on my service. Oddly, I never received a response. But it was just thrilling to send my photos to places like "Television City" or "Avenue of the Stars." And now, caressing a pair of Kinney shoes was gonna get me there.

The first thing that really struck me as I stepped off the plane in L.A. was the openness of it. Sky, sky, and more sky. I had had eight years of tromping along past the gray concrete of New York skyscrapers into the dark urine-soaked subways and back up to the concrete again. And there was always that guy who stood at the end of my street every day with fifty-two McDonald's coffee stirrers meticulously woven into his hair, saying robotically, "I'll take five dollars, please!" I never gave him five dollars. But I usually gave him something to ward off bad karma. I was only a shoe show away from that guy's life.

But L.A.—the sun hit me bright, like an egg-whites-only omelette. I felt like Lazarus! A huge weight that I hadn't even realized was there rose off my shoulders. My God, L.A.! Yes! And then there was the hotel. The Universal Registry. I'll never forget the name. All shiny and sparkling with brass fixtures and marble floors—and that was just the parking garage. When I got to my room, I could scarcely believe my eyes. For some reason I was given a huge corner suite, bigger than all my New York apartments put together. And a real bed, way up off the floor! Clean sheets, clean towels, and that bathroom—a TV and a phone next to the toilet. Talk about multitasking! And all those amenities. Little bottles of soaps, shampoo (no Pert), moisturizer, Q-tips, sewing kit, shoeshine cloth, lint brush—that room should have been declared the fifty-first state. The best part was that it wasn't costing me a dime. In fact, I was being paid to stay there and getting per diem on top of that. At that point, I would have *married* the shoes if the company had asked me to. My room overlooked the pool and the Jacuzzi, and, of course, everything was surrounded by those magical palm trees.

There were five of us in the "cast," and in two weeks we only had to do three "shows" that lasted about an hour and a half each. At night, the shoe company reserved a table for us in the back of the conference room, where we ate bad chicken Kiev and laughed our heads off. The big attraction at those dinners was the huge bucket of Coronas in the middle of the table. As soon as the sales managers started giving their speeches, we'd grab that bucket and head out to the pool and drink and swim under the stars of a beautiful L.A. night, the palm trees silhouetted black against the sky—heaven.

But back to those amenities. I discovered that if you took all the little bottles and kits and stuffed them in your suitcase, housekeeping would replace them the next day. And the next. And the next. For two weeks! By the time we finished the shoe tour, I had to buy another bag just to haul all that stuff back to New York. I arrived back in Hell's Kitchen tan, rich, and set for life, ablutions-wise. As I stepped into our dismal little place, I announced triumphantly to Donna, "We'll never have to buy shampoo again!"

Now I'm writing this from a hotel in Nova Scotia. It's a great hotel. And I am rather enjoying the peace and tranquillity, and the fact that there is a whole film crew catering to my every need. But I miss my husband and kids. Listen, I won't lie: hotels can be great escapes from real life. And lots of life can happen in and around hotels. It's where my husband and I had our first date. And where we conceived one of our boys. We stayed at the Berkeley in London to celebrate our new marriage, and ten years later we stayed at the Cipriani in Venice to revive it. We once tried to save money when we were out of work by booking us and the kids in one room, so every night we had to sit out on the balcony and stare at the parking lot, waiting for the boys to fall asleep, then we'd go back in and watch TV with the sound off.

I mean, there's no denying that it's great to leave your shoes outside your hotel room and find them polished in the morning, but it's more fun waking up to your two-year-old pulling all the shoes out of the cubbies to practice his counting. And though I enjoy having housekeeping clean my bathroom every day, I must admit that I was thrilled when young Joe refused to flush the toilet until I got home from work so he could show me how he pooped in the potty all by himself. The beauty of eggs Benedict served on a silver tray with a rose and the *Times* still sings its siren song, but I just can't hear it as well anymore over the clatter of breakfast dishes, bad knock-knock jokes, and on-the-way-to-school backseat fighting.

Now that I have a family, the best part of staying in a hotel is checking out. Because at the end of every day, you need to go home. It's where you want to be. It's where you should be. In the confusion, the craziness, the yelling, the spilled milk, the poopy diapers. Like Dorothy said, "There's no place like home." All right, everybody, click those ruby heels together and repeat after me . . .

I'll take the continental breakfast, egg-white omelette, fresh blueberries and yogurt, and chicken-and-apple sausage, with seven-grain toast and fresh-squeezed orange juice. Hold all my calls. Especially if you hear the Barney theme song in the background.

LOS
ANGELES

HOLLYWOOD COUPLES

YOU WANT TO KNOW WHY I think my husband, Dave, and I have a better than average chance (at least in Hollywood) of having a lasting (more than 13.5 years) marriage? First of all, we don't get along that well. We fight a lot. We're not very compatible, we don't have much in common, and we each have habits that drive the other person totally, nerve-nakedly insane.

We have different ideas about how we want to raise the boys, we regularly criticize each other's driving, and we can't even agree on what *country* to live in, for cryin' out loud! We have a talent for taking turns being too sensitive or not sensitive enough, so that one of us is always in a state of excruciating emotional agony. Or at least really pissed off. Each of us feels that we do *everything* around here and the other person does *nothing*. He thinks I spend too much money, I think he spends too much money, and we never get each other the right Christmas gift. We can't come to terms with how much sex is enough or not enough. And that's when the sex in question is zero.

The marriage workload—kids, career, no sex—is staggered in such a unique way that even with all our help we are both constantly exhausted, or "knackered," as Dave likes to say (I hate when he uses those quaint British expressions). The exhaustion leads to short tempers, and the tempers lead to fights, slamming doors, tears, and bitter recriminations—whatever recriminations are. The word just sounds perfect for how we feel after fighting.

Fairy-tale Hollywood couple, right?

Welcome to the grown-up world of marriage. One that you won't find that often in Lala Land. It's as rare in Hollywood as an Amish agent. More often than not, you'll read story after story about instant attraction, hugely romantic gestures, great sex. That's when I set my watch and give the relationship anywhere from three months to three years to fall apart. Because the greatest lesson I've learned lo these past eleven years of wedded blisters is that *you need to have a bit of contempt for the person you are about to marry.* You'd better have that contempt going into it, 'cause it's gonna show up sooner or later, and all those cute and quirky affectations you so adored in your fiancé become the red-hot needle in your eyeball down the road. And a red-hot needle in your eyeball can be quite a shock.

That's the problem with a lot of Hollywood couples. They think that finding each other sexy, brilliant, and hilarious means they're meant for each other! No, no, NO! They're all wrong! It's the exact opposite! Don't go for Cindee, the Malibu volleyball queen who graduated from the Cordon Bleu and just signed a million-dollar deal to design a line of lingerie—NO! Go for Gladys, the squat girl from the mall who eats her egg salad with her mouth open. Because eventually Cindee will turn into Gladys, and it's so much easier to know that going into it. Tristan might have had his book of poetry serve as the inspiration for this year's blockbuster movie, and maybe he did teach Tibetan orphans on his way back down from scaling Mount Everest (with no superficial oxygen), but at some point he'll be asking you to clean his nose-hair clippers and pop that weird thing on his back.

So why is it that in Hollywood, couples cavort and kiss in all the national magazines, cooing about how they feel spiritually connected, talking about gazing endlessly into each other's eyes, giggling about their pet names? They go public with the most outrageously naïve statements about love, marriage, and relationships, practically guaranteeing that the quotes will come back to bite them in the butt. Here are a few of the juicier ones I've read:

"We have so much in common, it's as if we are the same person." Uh-oh.

"Marriage is about the meeting of two minds and souls and hoping that it is going to work forever." Ouch.

"My reaction to meeting her was pure lust—totally physical. We had a sense of destiny." That's okay for now, pal, but just wait until she has that episiotomy.

"Marriage won't change my life." No comment.

Guess what happened to the marriages of all the originators of those comments? You got it.

Now, I don't fault these people for getting a divorce. Lots

of stuff goes on in a marriage that outsiders can't possibly know, and, hey, I had a prior three-year marriage myself. The difference is, I knew the first one was never going to work, and I was sure the same thing would happen this time. I went around to anyone who would listen, begging them to talk me out of going down the aisle again. And yet, with so many Hollywood couples, six months after a breakup they are with new "soul mates," spouting the same nonsense all over again. Have you ever wondered how this happens? Wonder no more! I can explain it all to you. Not that it's any big mystery. It's due to the magic of show business, the land where the line between illusion and delusion separates nothing.

You remember being in junior high school, with the full flush of first love infecting the entire eighth- and ninth-grade classes, right? That very same kind of heady blood rush and love lust still thrives on movie and television sets and in theaters to this day. They are artificial and temporary worlds where the actors have a hard time separating the roles they play on-screen from the reality off-screen, and the crew, out of boredom, have a hard time keeping their hands out of other people's pants. The atmosphere of a film set or a stage is not unlike high school, with popularity/power castes in which stars, costars, and directors tango in a dance of self- and mutual adoration.

Being a rich, successful actor in Hollywood, of any persuasion (gay, bi, or *whatever*), is like being on the best first date of your life, except that this first date can last for years, depending on how good your agent is. It's a first date with everyone in the world you ever wanted to meet. It's endless first-love infatuation with major money. Jet-setting to exotic islands, having your butt kissed in different languages, front-row seats, backstage passes, red carpet, first class, beef Wellington, free drinks, and a full body massage. Just imagine.

Throw in the fact that there's a whole industry dedicated to recording all of this photographically and printing it for the whole world to drool over and envy. And I must confess, I've been a party to that deception. Four years ago, when we were summering in England (which is the way the magazines would phrase it; we would phrase it as basically being stuck in a tiny house in the remote English countryside during the rainiest June and July Europe had ever experienced in recorded history—without a nanny), I found out that I was—surprise!—pregnant with our fourth.

Oh, the look on Dave's face. He then went into a catatonic shock for three days, sitting in front of the telly watching gardening shows and eating chocolate biscuits. Meanwhile, I was trying to feed, clothe, and entertain my brood without the convenience of a car. We footed it to the library, the bakery, and the duck pond every day (in the rain). Even if I could drive, there was nowhere to go, unless you count the coffee kiosk on the third floor of the little shopping mall in town. And the last thing I needed to give the kids was coffee.

Things finally came to a head when, trying to feed one, change another's diaper, and pull one off from around my neck, I yelled to Dave, as he slumped in the lounger, to find John's blanky. Without missing a beat (or getting out of his chair), he reached down, picked up the blanky, and threw it at me. That was it. My inner banshee was released and I went ape. I screamed at him to turn off the TV and practically knocked it off its stand. I grabbed him by the shirt with two hands and howled, "HELP ME WITH THE KIDS!!" I grabbed the baby and threatened to get on a plane back to L.A. with or without him. Dave's poor dear mother came rushing in and gasped, "You're scaring the children!"

As I collapsed onto the couch, trying to compose myself, the mail arrived, with a copy of *People* magazine in it, the theme being "Hollywood's Most Romantic Couples." And guess who had a centerfold Technicolor photo of themselves and their kidlings lounging peacefully and perfectly in the English countryside? Thaaat's right.

So I don't blame anybody, I don't point any fingers, except at my husband, Dave, who can sit and watch a cricket match (twice as long and three times as boring as baseball but without the stadium mustard) for six hours and then ask what we're having for dinner.

But I'm telling you, one more star or starlet talking about endless love and preordained bliss . . . poor bastards. They blather on about how they like the same movies and music and food and travel and beaches. And sex! They both love having sex—at the same time! Boy, I'd like to visit *that* planet! Their existence is so far from reality that they don't realize that dating prepares you for marriage and kids the same way watching television prepares you for running a marathon.

If you want to know if you're prepared for marriage and kids with a person, try *never* seeing any movies at all, *never* listening to your favorite music, and *never* eating at your favorite restaurant. And it will be about twenty years before you will travel the way you did when you were single. And sex? Forget about it. I mean that literally.

Then, how *do* you prepare for marriage? Unclear. The guests at my wedding all told me how moved they were by my tears as I wept throughout the ceremony. Should I have told them they were actually sobs of fear as I watched myself voluntarily walk into another oncoming train?

But I *can* tell you the exact moment I knew my marriage had a chance. We had almost not survived the first year (second worst year of my life, after my mother dying, and just *barely*), and we had just gotten through the birth of our first son, when the Great Christmas Flu of 1994 hit.

I have never experienced anything like it before or since. We were spending the holidays on our own in California with no family in sight. Two days before Christmas, little Sam became feverish, throwing up every hour, stopping only long enough to splash me with diarrhea. The poor thing! He was miserable. Dave and I were running around changing his compress and rewashing his crib sheets. Right around dinnertime Dave started to look flushed, and in no time flat I was making two compresses at a time and changing the crib and the bedsheets. Apparently I was too good at being Florence Nightingale, because around bedtime I was down for the count. Thus began the Long Night's Journey into Day.

We tried to retain some camaraderie, gamely trading off the baby to let the other one throw up or cramp up, but by three A.M., when Sam had finally fallen asleep, it was every man for himself. We went from "Honey, what can I get you?" to "Pass me the bucket—quick!" And since we had only two sets of sheets, by four A.M. we were passing each other in the hall, silent and naked, our eyes glazed over with fever, our breath reeking like roadkill, one on the way to put the soiled towels in the wash, the other with the last two clean dish towels to throw over the now-bare mattress.

Two days later we managed to recover enough to cook Christmas dinner for four friends. After grace, Dave lifted his glass and, gazing lovingly across the table, gave thanks for all his blessings and toasted me, his lovely bride. I thought, "Wait a minute. Just two days ago this guy saw me with greasy hair, purple circles under my eyes, and skid marks on the back of my jammies. Either he's legally insane or madly in love!"

I pick madly in love—and you can quote me on that.

TIME OUT

WHAT DOES IT MEAN when it's August and the almighty and magnificent grape Popsicle no longer solves all parental problems? It means it's time to get the kids back in school before Mom has to call Betty Ford.

On one particularly long, hot day I had picked up the little ones (who shall henceforward be known as "the other two") from pre-K primal-scream therapy (very big here in southern California). I was still left to deal with the ever-constant dilemma: what to do with four boys under eight years of age.

Normally, the pool is the most reliable summer-day shredder. There's nothing like a six-hour sun- and chlorine-bleaching to break the back of a way-too-long day. I learned this from my mom. Although having your own pool in suburban Cleveland was as rare as foxhunting, there were a couple of private swim clubs.

Now, our family was not the private-club type. I'm not trying to get "street cred" here or anything, but my dad, a sports-

Patricia Heaton

writer with five kids, five kids all attending Catholic school, was supporting us on about $350 a week and all the stadium hot dogs we could eat.

For the rich kids there was Aquamarine, which was the up-market resort-style swim club that had lifeguards who were actually certified. And where the kids could order food and "sign" for it. That killed us. To think you could summon pizzas, burgers, French fries, and chocolate shakes with your signature. What does *that* kid's dad do for a living? And where do I sign up?

We, on the other hand, belonged to a place called Water 'n' Stuff, which was a *teensy* bit less exclusive than Aquamarine. It had a big, suspiciously warm baby pool, and an expansive yard full of those little hard-to-see prickerweeds that made the lawn like a minefield.

There was a "swing set" (a metal frame cemented into the lawn with a single, lonely bucket swing) and a chrome and aluminum slide that became so hot in the summer sun it could give you third-degree burns, plus two slabs of smooth cement that had once been shuffleboard courts. You could kind of make out the pyramid scoring system if you got it wet and then knelt down and looked real close.

By the way, the most admired shuffleboard technique was always not only to knock your opponent's disk off the board but to make sure it slammed into your opponent's toes with a satisfying *crack*!

You had to pay attention or suffer the consequences.

Water 'n' Stuff was my mom's version of family Valium. She'd be fast asleep in her chair with a copy of Teilhard de

Chardin's *The Phenomenon of Man* covering her face while we blissfully played "underwater tea party" (me), did big belly flops off the diving board (my brother), peed in the pool, and played Flipper, based on the popular television show of the day, or Marco Polo (which I now realize is the world's most annoying game).

A particularly exotic touch at Water 'n' Stuff was that the snack bar kept all the candy bars in the freezer. Those 3 Musketeers were as hard as a winter sidewalk and could last all day. We used them as shuffleboard disks when we were low on cash.

They were also useful for removing those last few stubborn baby teeth. Of course, you couldn't "sign" for them. Sally Greene and I had to steal the change our brothers earned with their paper routes.

But now that I am on a television show out here in sunny California, sometimes known as Sony California, my family is required by law to have its own private pool. (No yard, you understand, but a big pool. Well, not that big. But it's ours. And we can keep non–TV stars out.)

But since my name isn't in the title of the television show, we can't afford a lifeguard. (A certain person in the show, for whom the sitcom is named, has lifeguards for his pool and linesmen for his tennis court. But I'm not bitter and there's no resentment.)

So I'm forced to sit out there feigning interest in the "Mom, watch this!" stuff (if you wear big sunglasses, it really looks like you're paying attention) and trying to get the kids to change Marco Polo's name.

But my kids were pooled out. They couldn't bear even the thought of any more water. So while I was trying to think up Plan B, I told the boys to go up to their bedrooms and clean their mess. This suggestion was met with great wailing and gnashing of teeth. (They tend to reserve the rending of garments for food groups they object to.)

Immediately I morphed into Miss Gulch and yelled, "Crying? I'll give you something to cry about!" It worked, sort of. I had to help pick up. As we were cleaning, I began to feel a bit peckish (*peckish* being a British word meaning "hungry." I picked it up from my British husband, Lord Nigel St. Crispenson-the-Thames by Crackey by Jove by Churchill. And you wonder why I kept my own last name).

I thought about taking them to Spago. "Who wants French fries and Brie?" No takers; they knew Spago was way too near Neiman Marcus and it would be hours before they could get slightly acquainted with a grilled portobello appetizer. And anyway, they can't keep a secret and my husband didn't buy my last explanation, that Spago was giving away a free pair of shoes with each entrée. ("Kinda like Happy Meals!")

I made a million suggestions for things to do, all to no avail. Bowling, tennis, the park—they all just whined. The fact was that all summer they had way too many arranged activities. I had signed them up for pottery, archery, science club, cooking—anything to fill up the day. There was the combined dread of having to deal with them all day and fear that if they didn't learn to needlepoint before the seventh grade, they wouldn't get into Yale.

The boys just didn't want to get in the car again and have

to go to something that felt suspiciously like school, to make some lame craft item that would just junk up the house but make Mom feel like she was getting her $250 worth.

I decided to leave them to their own devices. "Do what you want, I'm gonna clean out my office," I said as I walked away. I went down the hall and began to organize my files and clean out my drawers. One by one they wandered in. Sam found the atlas and asked how close England and their nana was to California. We started looking at the maps, and then got out the globe. That led to a discussion about planets, and John wanted to look through a telescope. We didn't have one, so we got the microscope out instead and decided to look at stuff through that. After we had looked at hair and spit, we went downstairs to see if we could find moldy bread. I hate to admit it, but we did. Before we brought it back upstairs to view it, we decided to make lunch, and then bake some brownies. They wanted to do the dishes, so I pulled some chairs up to the sink and they played around in the suds for a while.

Before we knew it, the day was done, and we had kind of wasted it. We puttered, talked, and goofed off, and I never got my office organized. But we had spent a whole day together. They asked questions, I answered the ones I knew, and we looked up the stuff I didn't. I showed them how to use a dictionary, how to surf the Internet, how to measure stuff. They cracked eggs, stuck paper clips to magnets, and played paper-triangle football.

I got to know my kids a little bit better, and they got to know me. I remembered how much I not only love my kids but really *like* them.

I recently read a book about how families in other countries spend their time. Most of the families featured in the book were poor and struggling, and after spending the day just trying to survive together, they relaxed in the evening by just being together.

What is it about living in a prosperous society that makes us spend more and more time apart from the ones we love? The more educated we are, the wealthier we become, the more we seem to isolate ourselves in our work in order to give our families the best of everything. When all we and our kids really want is the best of one another. And we'll even settle for less than the best. As long as we're together.

We do a lot more puttering these days. Although I still drag them to Spago for lunch occasionally.

They *love* those Brie French fries.

SURVIVAL JOBS:
PART III

I CAME TO LOS ANGELES with two advantages: some cash in my pocket, and an instinct that this was not the town in which to take a restaurant job.

Everyone knows that Hollywood is all about image, and the last image I wanted to project in this temple of youthful success was that of an aging (by L.A. standards) divorcée smelling of eggs Benedict, with cappuccino stains down her apron, pursuing that elusive Olive Garden commercial.

Now, don't get me wrong. I think commercials are the best thing going for actors. I had one or two running when I moved to Los Angeles, and they were the reason I was able to produce my own plays here. And there is many an actor making a mighty fine living just holding up a box of detergent.

But having spent most of my commercial residuals on my own productions, I was shortly in need of a job, and I wanted one that I could just hide in. Fortunately, there are enough windowless offices in this town for people like me to disappear in.

There are also many actors here who are generous and openhearted, willing to share their survival tips with a fellow thespian. That was not always the case in New York. There are so few jobs there, and it is such a closed and rather cliquish and rarefied circle, that people tend to be more guarded and stingy with their information.

Los Angeles, on the other hand, still has a bit of the Wild West about it: plenty of opportunity for all, awash with energetic, optimistic pioneers whose sense of impending bounty fills them with a glorious generosity of spirit. Or maybe they're just naïve and stupid from all the coke and Ecstasy. In any case, I always found someone who was willing to help me out, give me a phone number, or refer me to a friend.

That's how I landed at DepoSums. DepoSums is one of those niche industries that is a small but important cog in the Great Scheme of Things. An actor friend told me about *his* actor friend who was in charge of hiring at DepoSums, a legal service that summarized depositions for law firms with overburdened caseloads. All you needed to know was how to read and type.

So, I never thought I would say it, but thank God for Mr. Hale, my high school typing teacher. He was a benign and imperturbable man who I hated every Monday, Wednesday, and Friday at 2:40 when he hit his stopwatch and said, "Go!" Those typing tests drove me crazy: I couldn't stand the pressure and I always did poorly, and yet right now I'm zipping along on my keyboard, typing this book, and eight years ago I was supporting myself nicely at DepoSums.

DepoSums was somewhat of an oasis for me. I felt slightly more intelligent, working at a law-related company, and the other summarizers were the greatest bunch of wackos I'd ever met. We all sat in a little room, we out-of-work actors, writers, and directors, like broken toys on the Island of Misfit Angelenos. A lot of the cases we were summarizing were fascinating, and often the tedium of the day was relieved every half hour or so by someone shouting, "Oh, my God, listen to this!" and then reading out loud some horrifying tabloidlike story from a deposition.

One of the best ones I ever heard was the case of the physician who was being sued by a Hispanic family because he had accidentally severed the vas deferens of their only son during some routine medical procedure. Doc didn't tell the family about this little unintentional alteration, and his helpful daughter, who worked in his office, doctored the kid's files so that it wasn't recorded.

The daughter had felt it necessary to cover for her dad; she didn't want him to be sued and lose his practice, because then she couldn't *embezzle* from him anymore to support *her* drug habit.

Wow. If Hollywood producers only knew. All they have to do is get their lackeys a temp job at a law firm, and they'd have endless movie material. That particular case kept our little office engrossed for weeks.

Reading the testimony of these characters—the newly recovering junkie daughter, the arrogant doctor, the hysterical family—to all my coworkers was like gathering all your best friends to watch your favorite soap. And when things weren't so interesting, we'd while away the time mocking one another mercilessly.

My new best friend in L.A., Dewey, had done a few small but significant parts in major motion pictures, but was going through a dry spell and came aboard at DepoSums. I saved her butt and showed her the ropes, and never let her forget that even though she was a semi–big shot out there in the real world, inside this joint my word was law. (Translation: Would she mind lending me seventy-five cents so I could get a Pay-Day out of the candy machine?)

Oh, and another thing about DepoSums. My husband proposed to me there.

I had broken up with him while he was in New York (I know, that was cowardly of me), and apparently it goosed him enough to buy a ring, get on a plane, and fly to L.A. with a proposal.

I was sitting at my desk, summarizing away, a Walkman on my head blasting the B-52's, when I felt a tap on my shoulder. There was Lord Crackers and Cheese, a wild look in his eye, asking me to walk down to the courtyard with him. He did the whole bit—down on one knee, little black box in his jacket, proper proposal. The thing that kept me from saying yes right away (it took about five minutes) was that I was thinking about how I spent the night before.

It had been with Dewey, and after chewing her ear off about how much better I felt now that I was single, we went through her address book to see who she could fix me up with. I had sworn to her that I had learned my lesson and was through with actors, and she assured me she had all kinds of nonactor types available for introductions.

And now I was heading back up to the office with Dave on

one hand and an engagement ring on the other. We walked into our little room, and before Dewey could say a word I shouted out, "Dave asked me to marry him and I said yes. Isn't that GREAT?!" I stared daggers at Dewey's startled, then disgusted, face, and, being a friend, she behaved graciously until she got me alone later. I'm still paying for wasting her precious evening.

My singlehood may have ended that day, but the depositions didn't. I decided to take the thing a step further and purchased my own computer so that I could work at home. That way I could summarize on my own time, and shape my day the way I wanted to. Much as I missed the office, auditions were coming in, and I needed to be available.

That meant summarizing at two, three in the morning. Which was doable. A bit dangerous, though. When one has been typing for six hours straight (starting at midnight) on a case that involves a Japanese ball bearing manufacturing company, one tends to get light-headed and forgets to save one's document as one goes along. And then when one deletes the whole thing accidentally at eight A.M., one cannot go to that Fourth of July barbecue one has been looking forward to all week.

Instead, one starts the whole damn five-hundred-page document all over again.

That's why doing commercials is a much better deal, if you can score one. And I did score a few in L.A. You have to go on a million auditions to get even close to snagging one, unless you are a well-known fixture on the commercial circuit. But one or two days' work on a national commercial can keep you afloat for a year or more. Thank God for residuals.

And commercials are almost like acting. That's another wonderful aspect of L.A. The survival gigs in this town can make you feel like you are actually in show business! No wonder people stick it out here for so long. You can do a couple of commercials, perhaps a week on a TV show, and you're financially set for that year. It's not exactly a career, but it pays the bills. With very little effort. At least the actual work itself doesn't take much effort. *Getting* the job is another story.

So I entered into a phase of survival work that looked a little bit like a career. To my family, anyway. I knew my bit part on *Matlock* was not a career move, just a paycheck. Especially with the hairdo they gave me. The women doing the hair on that show looked like they had just finished a tour of duty with Ann Miller. Lots of hairspray, lots of blue eye shadow. They eyed me suspiciously when I declined their offer to back-comb me.

It was a thrill to be seen by all the folks back in Cleveland when I got the part on *Matlock*. It was my aunt Jane's favorite, God rest her soul. But I knew it for what it was—a paycheck and a little bit more tape for my very short actor's reel. The show was also a graveyard for other actors who had hit it big awhile ago and now were back down in the trenches with the rest of us.

There were plenty of shows where an actor could go to die—*Murder, She Wrote; Love Boat;* and the one I was around for, *Alien Nation*. At least I played a human on that, so I didn't have a four A.M. makeup call. The downside was that I was recognizable. Well, almost. For some reason, though I was playing a doctor, I had a scene in which I was dressed in a purple suit with a *matching purple hat*. (Note to self: don't put myself in the care of any doctor who wears suits with matching hats.)

The director was some frustrated hack who was very impatient with me for no reason, and the topper was that my character ended up in a body bag. It's a bit spooky playing a dead person. Especially when they zip you in. What was even spookier was that I kind of liked it. Being dead. Never mind.

I also scored a couple of survival roles in feature films. What a great way to make a living. When you're single and childless. If you actually have a life, being on a feature film can be really boring and tedious. Unless you're the star. Hasn't happened to me yet. But as a survival gig, it's terrific, and you never know what childhood icon you'll be sitting next to in the makeup chair.

Like Chevy Chase.

When we were in high school, Sally Greene and I used to stay up late together the first year *Saturday Night Live* aired, and twenty years later I'm cast in *Memoirs of an Invisible Man* and I'm up all night trying to figure out what I should call him when I see him in the morning—"Mr. Chase?" "Chevy?" (Hard *ch* or soft?) I end up staring straight ahead and ignoring him when he walks in, because I so can't believe that I'm working with the guy who I used to stay up until midnight to watch with Sally Greene and a root beer float.

And what about the director of that film? John Carpenter. When I was living in New York, I went to see his remake of *The Thing* by myself because I was the only one I knew who liked that kind of thing. Me and four other people in a Times Square movie theater at two o'clock in the afternoon. I figured

I should get the phone numbers of the other four people in the theater so that we could attend these events together. At any rate, I loved *The Thing* and I couldn't wait to work with him.

After a few minutes on the set, I realized that John Carpenter had never really worked with human beings, just monsters. Because his only direction was to say, "Actors, tense up for acting!" That was about the gist of it.

Of course, I was the nerdy day player on the set, who was trying to do deep background work on a character who basically had two lines. I barely got a close-up on that movie, but I still love *The Thing*.

The joy of that job was working with Michael McKean, who was funny and nice, and Daryl Hannah, who was beautiful and thoughtful. Let me just mention this about Daryl: I worked only for about four days on that film, and yet she offered me her dressing room if I wanted to watch movies with her on her VCR, and she gave me a completely unwarranted gift of a T. Coraghessan Boyle book when I wrapped on the movie. It was a lesson to me about how the most seemingly insignificant gesture of kindness can make a difference in someone's life.

Friends back in New York and Cleveland figured I had it made. They'd see me here and there in something, and thought I was living the high life. And yet there I would be, wiping my makeup off from a day of filming, and sitting down to summarize 350 pages of *Jarndyce* v. *Jarndyce*.

The little bits of work *were* encouraging, but I had met a lot of people who floated around in that no-man's-land of bit parts, so I wasn't kidding myself—I knew I had a long way to go.

I had actually just about reached the end of my rope with

the whole show-business thing. I was getting a little bit of work, but after so many years, the payoff seemed pretty paltry, and I had eight times as many rejections as I had job offers. I set the timer—I would give myself about another year in L.A., and then start contemplating another line of work.

Right around that time I went on a trip to Mexico with my church, First Presbyterian of Hollywood. They support an orphanage in Tecate called Sparrow's Gate, and they were off to lay down some sod at the facility so that the kids would have a lawn to play on. I roped my then-fiancé, Sir Marmite St. Beans-on-Toast, to go with me, and there proceeded to have one of the true epiphanies of my life.

A bunch of us from the church set off in two vans to the border, and a more motley crew could not be imagined. We drove to Mexico and somehow found the orphanage, which was just outside Tijuana. It was a humble collection of stucco buildings run by a very hardworking couple, Dale and Alba Tinney. They wasted no time in putting us to work fixing a sewage pipe, prepping the hard, dry patch of ground for the sod, and generally hanging with the kids.

We divided our time between hard manual labor and playing around with the kids, who were excited just to have us there as a diversion. I don't speak Spanish, so there was a lot of plain old playing ball and running around.

At night we slept in little bunkers on cots. There was no television, radio, or phone, except for emergencies. We laid sod, threw the kids a party, had a church service, went into Tijuana for beer and steak, and then headed back to L.A.

That trip did something to me. As I lay in the little room I was renting in a house in West Hollywood, I felt something I hadn't felt in all my past years of struggle—peace. That weekend in Mexico—the forced media deprivation, the physical labor, the openness and simplicity of those kids—had changed something inside me. I felt totally released from the need to make it as an actress. I had experienced complete fulfillment in something that had nothing to do with me being in the spotlight. In fact, it was the exact opposite. It was about being involved in something that *wasn't* about me. Hmmm.

So, just at the time I knew I could walk away from this whole acting thing, I started working regularly. Just when I was ready to throw it all away, it was all thrown my way. And I can only conclude that the whole cosmic plan as it concerned me was to put success in perspective. Mexico taught me that my life was all about my connection to others, whether I was working on a set or in a field. It wasn't about the job; it was about how I did the job, and how I viewed the people I met on the job.

As I said, I started working fairly regularly after that. And I haven't had to take any survival jobs for a few years. Not that I believe for a minute that I'm home free. My fifteen minutes will be up shortly, and I'll be scrounging around for something to do in a few years. My next survival job won't look like my former ones; but I'll give you a little hint—when you see me hawking my own line of age-defying beauty products on the Home Shopping Network, you'll know.

And when you hear me say "It really works!" have a little pity and buy some. I'll take Visa or MasterCard.

SOME THINGS THAT
HAVING MONEY DOESN'T CHANGE

1. Having or being an idiotic spouse.
2. Your breath in the morning.
3. Kids crying.
4. The idiot driving 35 mph in the fast lane in front of you talking on the cell phone.
5. Catching colds.
6. Bad weather.
7. Insomnia.
8. Your favorite baseball team losing three straight to the Yankees at home.
9. The inexplicable popularity of tattoos.
10. People talking in movie theaters.
11. Airlines losing your luggage. Even when you haven't flown anywhere in years. The bastards come to your house, grab your luggage, and send it to Bora-Bora.
12. The inability to decline that third slice of pizza.
13. That big zit in the middle of your forehead.

14. No matter where you live, or how secluded and private and protected you think yourself to be, never being able to escape the ad campaign for cellular phone companies.
15. Your hard drive crashing.
16. Certain sitcom actors farting on the set.
17. Having to stop for gas when you're late for work.
18. Kids playing music really loud in their cars, hoping you'll respond crabbily, like your constipated and almost eighty-two-year-old uncle. Which you do.
19. The cardboard subscription inserts in magazines.
20. Voice-mail menus.
21. Children throwing up without warning.
22. Waking up to find there's no cream for the coffee.
23. Getting your period.
24. Breaking out before getting your period.
25. Having to buy Girl Scout cookies.
26. Flushing floaters left by forgetful children.
27. Picking up laundry off the stairs.
28. Wiping the kitchen countertop eight hundred times a day.
29. The express checkout at the grocery store always taking longer than the regular line.
30. People asking for your autograph and then being bitterly disappointed that you're not Valerie Bertinelli.
31. Realizing you're going to die anyway.
32. Needing glasses.
33. Being unable to find parking almost daily.
34. Picking up the toys.
35. Running out of toilet paper.
36. Parent-teacher conferences.

37. Having to send out Christmas cards.
38. Soccer snacks.
39. Monkey balls. (Just threw that in there to see who's paying attention.)
40. Getting old.

ACTING AWARDS: TOTALLY AND UTTERLY MEANINGLESS (UNTIL YOU WIN A COUPLE)

HERE WE GO AGAIN. The pain, the agony, the humiliation—the Emmy Awards. In Hollywood, you can always tell when there's an awards show coming up. The town goes into weight-loss overdrive. And not just the usual cocaine and sour-apple-martini plan. No, it's the much more drastic Zone diet torture. This is the diet where they hand-deliver minuscule slices of beef and microscopic portions of egg-white frittatas to you for a mere fifty bucks a day. Once you get over the headaches and dizziness, you melt away until you're all bones and hardened arteries, then you get stinking drunk at the after-parties because you lost (or won), and the diet doesn't allow you to eat after six so you drink . . . but I get ahead of myself.

Did I ever imagine there would come a day when I hated trying on evening gowns? I guess I never imagined evening gowns as a part of my daily existence at all. But I used to love dress-up. My mom had one silky, satiny bathrobe that I loved to put on, after which I would pretend I was a captive princess on a pirate ship, and the pirates had me tied to a mast, and they would—well, that's another book. The one my therapist will write. My name will be disguised as Hatricia Peaton.

But Suzie (with the long hair) Albertz's mom had a steamer trunk of nightgowns, costume jewelry, and these tiny samples of Avon eye shadow that were the size of little bullets stacked on top of each other. (I was partial to olive green and lots of it!) She used to let us rip through her stuff, get all dolled up, then run around the backyard playing Grecian goddess. She didn't even mind when I fell and got grass stains all over her negligee. Back then, I felt gorgeous!

Cut to Los Angeles, 2000. My stylist Ricci (as in "Ricky," but the L.A. version) and I are standing in front of two racks of designer misogyny. But it's free (for one night), so who can complain, right? Well, let me. These gowns are all samples that have gone down a runway in New York or Paris on a model twenty-five years younger, two feet taller, and fifty pounds lighter than me. I've been to exactly one runway show, and take it from me, these chicks are really not from this planet. The white ones look like they're the offspring of a giraffe who mated with one of those aliens from *Close Encounters* and the black ones are all Venus Williams. And I'm the five-foot-two runt with four C-sections and too many years of nursing who's supposed to select one of these outfits to appear on television in front of millions of people. Thank you very much.

Now, I know there are such things as girdles and Wonderbras to give a gal a bit of help, but since all these gowns are strapless, backless, cut down to here, slit up to there, sheer

Lycra stretch-cling fabric, the only camouflage usable is possibly Band-Aids over your nipples, that is if you can find Band-Aids big enough to go over those babies since they went all platter-sized from nursing those ungrateful little . . . well, hell, it really doesn't matter because your nipples are actually pointing south, and if you just tape them down around your waist you'll have that nice flat-chested look that's so popular with the young people today. Hi, Gwyneth!

The other way to go is to pick the big beaded thing that looks like it came straight from last year's DAR convention. That's usually my choice. These gowns weigh about a thousand pounds, but they allow for an entire team of architects to erect scaffolding under there.

The really sick thing about the Emmys is that they are scheduled early in September, just after I've come back from four months of vacation. *Vacation* meaning "I'm off to England to eat my way through the British countryside with my husband, Lord Bangers and Stout for Breakfast!" There's the ten pounds that the camera adds, plus the ten pounds that the strawberries with clotted cream added, plus the ballast created by the double-stuffed Oreos dipped in peanut butter (completely worth it, by the way), plus beer. Did I mention beer already? And thus, the Zone diet.

Now, I've always loved meat. But that was before it became the only thing on the menu. Oh, and zucchini. Lots of zucchini on the Zone. I hate zucchini. (Why is it that neighbors who plant vegetable gardens only seem to plant tomatoes and zucchini? They plant way more than they could possibly ever eat, and then, smilingly, beneficently, give you twelve a week for three months. Maybe the fact that I have four kids makes people think I can use all this zucchini. But c'mon. The only vegetable I can get my boys to eat is potato chips.) But for six weeks I hang in there with this godforsaken diet. For six weeks I have no bread. Not a roll, not a bagel, not a cookie. No ce-real, no rice, no nothin'. Didn't lose a pound.

Now, it probably would have helped if I had exercised just a little bit. And at my age, that's the only thing that will guar-antee weight loss. Hard, long hours of gut-wrenching exercise works; that or plastic surgery. Which is what I opt for. Which is why I couldn't exercise. Yep, under the knife for no good reason other than sheer, unadulterated vanity. That stomach had to go. It wasn't even a stomach anymore, really. It was more like a big old wrinkly suede bag hanging down, accented with a herniated belly button on a career of its own. Not to mention the ridge of scar tissue below from the four C-sections. When I tried to suck it in, it just got all the more wrinkly, like one of those cute Chinese dogs with all the folds around their necks, except without the cute. And as I don't expect to have more kids biologically, I decided I'd had it with the kangaroo costume.

So off to my new best friend, the plastic surgeon, Dr. Hack-ensack. Not only does Hackensack do a bang-up job, I get to stay in a recovery center for three days and take Percocet, Valium, and Ambien *all at the same time.* That's right! Who knew? It was as if cutting me open, sewing my muscles back together, creating a new belly button, and scraping out seven years of scar tissue never happened! I woke up and there I was—Britney Spears! Of course there was a bit of discomfort, but it was just the same as a cesarean, so it was like greeting an old friend.

Now, would I have gone through all this if I wasn't an actress, if I didn't have a huge awards show to attend? Hard to say. I've been pretty vain-slash-insecure all my life, so maybe plastic surgery was always in my future. Well, the future is here!

And what a difference it has made for those evening-gown fittings! Not only can I skip the girdle, I can skip underwear altogether! *Yahoo!* And my stylist, Ricci, can stop searching for ways to make me look better, like "Try putting your shoulders back" or "Maybe I can find a higher heel" or, when all else fails, "People will understand—you've had four kids, for godsakes!"

So the fittings are relatively painless now; the next hurdle is the shoes. And the jewelry. And the bag, and the wrap, and the hair and makeup. Does all this sound shallow? Probably. But have *you* ever ended up in the "Don't" section of a fashion article? I lived there for two years.

It takes about three hours to put the whole thing together on the day. Glamorous? Perhaps. But since the Emmys happen on a Sunday, that morning consists of rounding up all my reluctant boys for church, sitting through my Sunday school class daydreaming about winning, hauling everyone home, getting them lunch, then sitting in my dining room in my bathrobe in front of the big picture window (better light), looking like one of those hookers on display in Amsterdam while makeup artist Brett gets out the plaster of Paris and tries to do something with the front of my head. They're not called makeup *artists* for nothing.

Friends and well-wishers stream in and out, and last year I even had a total stranger, a nine-year-old girl, actually Rollerblade through my front door (I really need to define my boundaries better). Funny, I had always pictured that day to start with me luxuriating in a rose-petal bubble bath, a glass of champagne in my hand, listening to light classical music or smooth jazz whilst receiving bouquets of flowers from fans. But even without that, somehow it does all come together, and I'm finally ready for that great limo ride into the unknown.

Did I mention my husband in all of this? Yes, he's actually around and actually has to look presentable, and after all the bow-tie trauma he ends up miserably holding my handbag in the background while the paparazzi shoot me. I sometimes think he wishes they would. Or him.

Which brings us to the show before the show—the Red Carpet. For all my complaining, it's a pretty heady experience. The minute you step out of your limo, your name is announced and hordes of fans start screaming. If you're lucky. Unlucky is when you arrive at just around the same time as, say, Julia Roberts, and then you might as well be wearing your Catholic school uniform for all the attention people will be paying *you.*

But eventually there's a lull and someone will notice you are there, and then you get to be queen for a day (or a few minutes). It would be nice if some of the reporters could think up some new questions. ("Patricia, you work full-time and have four children—how do you do it?") Or it would be nice if I would just be brave enough to answer truthfully. ("Well, I rarely see my kids, which is just the way I like it!") Those reporters must be truly bored out of their skulls to have to see the same people and ask the same questions year after year— one of the reasons I got out of journalism myself, which had originally been my college major. After about one semester of covering the fraternity beat, I realized I was way too self-involved to be interested in other people. Which is a terrible quality for a human being, but works well for a Hollywood television actress.

The awards themselves are like a different world altogether—a mind reader's brain would explode like a watermelon dropped off a ten-story building absorbing the thoughts of this crowd. I find myself constantly on edge as I sit in my seat, fighting a huge emotional battle—trying not to care, trying not to look like I care, trying to be okay with the fact that I care way too much. All this with a camera on me (ohmygod, did he catch me picking my nose?!). Now, there's some acting!

The struggles that are going on in that auditorium for those two hours are so embarrassingly painful that I have nothing but pity for all of us. No wonder it makes such good television. Why not bring back bearbaiting?

Raymond is a regular loser at these things, so there is some resignation on our parts even as we arrive. We're like Charlie Brown, faithfully kicking the football Lucy is holding for us, thinking maybe this year she won't pull it away. But there it is—flat on our backs again. We're the uncool lunch table at Hollywood High School.

In 2000, the impossible happened. I won the Emmy for Best Actress in a Comedy. It was my own Super Bowl, my own Kentucky Derby, my own World Series. It was, for me, beyond the beyond. Can I talk about winning? All I can say is that every single person on this planet should have the experience once in their life—it is the most fabulous, wonderful, exciting, thrilling, outrageously phenomenal feeling in the whole universe, even if it is completely meaningless. Only my children's births were more exciting (and I'm sticking that in here only because otherwise I'll look like a shallow jerk—I don't even *remember* my kids being born).

And then, let's throw in Cher as my presenter! Cher! Me, getting the highest honor in my field of work from CHER! And then, the next year, from Mary Tyler Moore! MTM! Could I have asked for more? I think if everyone once in their life got a big universal bear hug for doing what they do (from Cher! and Mary!), there would be no more war. For at least two weeks. 'Cause that's about how long the feeling lasts. But it's the best two weeks of your life! Needless to say, because God loves me so much and is highly concerned about the state of my soul, my bubble was burst almost immediately. No, not because I still had to get up with the kids the next morning at seven A.M. and feed them breakfast and dress them and drive them to school—not that. No, it was at the big Emmy party immediately after the awards, when an agent from *my* agency was introduced to me and, after hearing my name, said, "And what do *you* do?" You'd have thought that the Emmy in my hand would have given him a clue as to *what I do* (I win Emmys, you moron!). I actually still have the Emmy in my hand right now as I type this with the other.

But you see, right there, that's proof of God's existence—or His twisted sense of humor. Because the really important things in life are your family and friends. And what will people say about you at your funeral—that you won an Emmy once, or that you were a good person, kind and generous? Well, as for me, I hope it's the latter. And the fact that I recently commissioned an Emmy-shaped coffin just eliminates the need for anyone to bring it up.

Thank you and good night.

READING, WRITING,
AND LUNATIC

I HEARD SOMETHING the other day that made me think I should drain my pool, fire my personal trainer, and get outta town. There was an elementary school fund-raiser here in L.A. in which one of the auction items was a dinner for twenty in the winner's home prepared by none other than the world-famous chef Wolfgang Puck. The bidding *started* at $5,000 and ended up at $20,000. Because another parent wanted it so desperately, Wolfie generously decided he would do two private dinners at a mere $19,500 apiece.

That's *elementary* school, may I remind you.

WHAT WORLD AM I LIVING IN? Is it me, or is this really what it takes to teach your kid the three R's—readin', ritin', and *risotto con langosta*? Not to mention coloring inside the lines. Now, granted, this particular school, The Place for Rich Families to Display Their Unseemly Wealth in the Guise of Wanting What's Best for Their Child, or simply The Place, did reject my son when we applied, but I'm not bitter and there's no resentment. However, I do think there are some slightly rather alarming aspects to this trend.

First of all, what is being taught at a school that requires auctioning off Mel Gibson's underpants from *Braveheart*? (By the way, I didn't think they wore butt-wrap under those kilts.) Nuclear physics? And who put up the jack for the vegetarian karate lessons from Drew Barrymore and the David Hockney watercolor series of Michael Jackson's noses three through seven? Where did the school *get* Mel's underpants, and just what does the winner intend to do with them? (Hello, eBay! Smithsonian, line two!) Now, in its defense, The Place does take underprivileged and scholarship kids. They run the valet parking. But do you really want to be the welfare case at a school where the "What I Did on My Summer Vacation" essay from the kid sitting next to you begins: "Dr. Kissinger said the Nazi gold might be difficult to locate as our boat cruised along the jungle banks of the Amazon River. But he had a *hunch*."

Okay, I'll admit it—my kids do go to a private school, St. We're Not Catholic but You Can See Them from Here. And it's my own fault that Sammy wasn't admitted to the Place. In our final interview, the admittance counselor asked, "Where would you like to see Samuel by the sixth grade?" I answered, "Well, I would like him to have a sense that God loves him and a real heart for serving others," and as I blathered on I could see the woman's eyes glaze over. As I stumbled and stuttered to a close, she finally put me out of my misery. "No, I mean what college do you have him targeted for? Harvard or Yale?" Since I rarely think beyond my next manicure, I couldn't answer her. My first thought in that direction was that he could probably get into Ohio State as I had, drink a lot of beer, eat pizza, and maintain a C-minus average.

I hadn't a clue what the other schools were, plus I've always hoped that Jesus would come back before my kids got into middle school, thereby saving me from having that sex talk with them.

I guess I shouldn't be so shocked. When I became pregnant with Sam, I was told I had better start applying to schools for him. There was a place on the applications where you could attach the kid's ultrasound photo. Most of the schools that were recommended were miles from where we lived and had either tree names (Oaktree, Willowtree, and the one we could afford, Paltree) or futuristic ones, like Technolust Institute. My husband and I were both out of work at the time, and the tuition at these schools cost more than our agents could steal from us in a good year.

It's one of the few times I've looked back wistfully on my childhood. It seems to be getting better all the time. My grade school, St. Raphael's, was about a three-minute walk from our house. Suzie Albertz and I would stroll over in our blue plaid wool uniforms every day for eight years. Simple. No fuss, no cuss. You went to school where you lived. It just depended on what kind of licker you were. Catholickers turned left at the end of the street; publickers turned right.

That was about it. No gala fund-raisers, no after-school activities. At St. Raphael's we had a huge expanse of gravel and tar (generously called a playground) with a couple of swing sets, some basketball hoops (minus the nets), and a gray metal Maypole that could launch a second-grader into another county. And often did.

I remember selling Turkey Raffle tickets, a book of five for a dollar, where the grand prize was—you guessed it—a turkey. And then there was the annual bake sale to raise money for the missions. But generally school was a pretty hands-off proposition for parents. My dad sold some of the Turkey Raffle tickets at work and my mom made some brownies from the box for the bake sale. Obligation satisfied.

Today there are more organizations and subcommittees at Kids Catholic Lite Prep than I can shake my checkbook at. There's the Book Fair, Hot Dog Day, Doughnut Sales, Stock Market Simulation, the Newsletter Committee, Room Mothers, Library Helpers, Soccer League, Soccer Snacks, Story Hour, Indian Guides, Field Trip Chaperones, Grandparents Appreciation Committee, and, of course, the dreaded Silent Auction Chairperson.

Besides paying a monthly tuition that could feed all the Baldwin brothers for a year, there are all these extras. And as financially draining as all these activities are, having to participate myself is like adding insult to bribery. I mean, after all, isn't the best part of school paying people to take your kids out of your house for six hours a day? I've already *been* to school. I don't want to be at their school three days a week. As it is, my husband and I are working two jobs just to *afford* the frickin' place. We can't be expected to *attend* the place too. What kind of racket is this? You pay a fortune to send your kids to a private school and the school requires you to show up every day. It's like paying someone else to allow you to home-school your kids.

All right, enough. There's somebody at the door. Hopefully it's Jesus.

Hold your horses, I'll be right *there*, for crying out loud.

I CONFESS—GUILTY AS CHARGED—
HANGING IS TOO GOOD FOR ME

ONE OF THE SPECIAL PERKS that go along with lucking into a role on a top-ten-rated television show is that you become fresh meat and fair game for the tabloids.

I never thought in a million years I would qualify for one of these "a source close to the actress says" stories, wherein something horribly personal and embarrassing is revealed about me, my family, my marriage, or the five-thousand-dollar-a-day heroin habit I've kept hidden since the third grade. (It's not easy coming up with five large a day when you're in the third grade. *And* have milk money left over.)

You have to hand it to these tabloidians (but not without rubber gloves) that when they deem you in the interest of their readers, they will find a way to write a story about you. Even if it happens to be collected and cobbled together from the most remote and unreliable reaches of the showbiz universe.

My husband got there first, actually. He was shooting a

movie in Florida with Burt Reynolds, and some pictures from the set shot with a telephoto lens appeared on the cover of one of those fish wrappers. There was actually no "scandahl" attached to it; just some photographer who happened to be in a tree making a few bucks. The graininess of long-range photos tends to imply something less than tasteful going on, which is enough for these papers.

We were thrilled! The fact that the photos were there meant my husband was inching onto someone's radar. I was so jealous.

I didn't have to wait long.

Unfortunately, my first appearance in a tabloid ended up being a "Don't" in one of their fashion pages—I use the word *fashion* with some reserve. There was a photo of me looking the best I ever have—thin, tan from head to toe, wearing a tiny slip of a cocktail dress that only a truly fabulous person could get away with. According to this tabloid's fashion "expert," I had made the unforgivable mistake of not wearing *stockings*—I mean, first of all, who calls them stockings anymore? Next thing you know they'll be saying I applied too much *rouge*.

But second, what a relief! I couldn't have been happier. Because I knew that only hip, confident Hollywood types dared to venture out in bare legs, because they can—nothing to hide, just perfectly sculpted gams. I was in! And that was in the days before I had to pay a stylist thousands of dollars to tell me this.

The next time I made the papers, it wasn't about me. Or at least all of me. It was just about part of me. My breasts, to be exact. Full page, two photos—of my breasts. Supposedly a before-and-after composite. The article included a "renowned" plastic surgeon (Titz-R-Us) commenting on the photos, pointing out that the right breast was higher than the left breast, indicating some surgical work. I'm gonna let you in on a big secret. There's these things we gals in Hollywood use called push-up bras. You may have heard of them. You might have seen them advertised. You most likely have a minimum of eight of them in your underwear drawer. But don't let the guys know. It's good to keep a little mystery in the relationship.

And by the way, if those don't do the trick, pick up a pair of those "chicken cutlets," the silicon slices wrapped in plastic that you drop into your bra—pretty darn effective, real to the touch, but easily confused with actual cutlets, so be warned. Someone I know accidentally tried to grill hers and wound up giving her frying pan an extra coating of Teflon.

Now, this is not to say that I never had *any* work done on my two little friends, Cagney and Lacey. However, I had stuff *removed*, not added. See, after nursing four boys in rapid succession, my poor breasts were a mere shadow of their former selves: two empty flesh sacks plaintively *whap-whap-whapping* against my chest on my morning jog. Every time I had to be fitted in a gown, those babies had to be folded up like origami, tucked this way and that to fit into a strapless bra. My clothing stylist, Ricci, is a magician, but not a miracle worker. The day he held up a turtleneck muumuu for me to try on, insisting that the comeback of the "Maude" look was just around the corner and that I could be the first one to get in on it, was the day I knew it was time for the knife.

An added benefit after that surgery was that my waist size decreased, because I no longer had to tuck my breasts into my belt.

Of course the other area that the tabloids like to get wrong, really wrong, is the supposed conflicts on the sets of movies and shows. The week after I won my first Emmy, a story came out about how I was flaunting my little gold statuette, parading it around the stage, talking endlessly about my win, and generally being insufferable. The part they got *wrong* was that the rest of the cast was bitter, jealous, and resentful. Nothing was further from the truth. I mean, yes, they felt their lives were now empty and meaningless, but they didn't blame *me* for it.

Last year a tabloid did a story about the alleged daily depression I experience that causes constant and uncontrollable bouts of paralyzing sobbing due to my mother's death when I was twelve years old. Again, it was another cut-and-paste job, quotes from a Lifetime special added to things I told Marilyn Beck about a TV movie I did.

Now, I don't think it's too self-indulgent to admit that when your mom dies when you are twelve it can cause a kind of sadness that has a way of staying with you. But to imply that it has caused incapacitating depression? It's being married, having four kids, and working forty hours a week that causes the uncontrollable sobbing.

The surefire way I know that these papers are making stuff up is when they write that a source close to me told them that "Pat" said this or that. Nobody calls me Pat. Nobody close to me, anyway. I had the great idea that all I needed to do was track down this person who calls me Pat and I'd have found the leak. I suddenly noticed that our props guy, Don Rosemond, called me Pat occasionally. And he was always coming in with brand-new tennis shoes. I hear those tabloids pay really well . . . Don denies everything.

Ultimately, it's a no-win situation with these papers. If I complain, it only makes the allegations seem more authentic. If I sue, it costs a fortune. If I do nothing, the terrorists win. I mean the tabloidians.

I figure there's only one way to go: confess. Confess to everything. I did it. And if I haven't done it, I *will* do it. At least this way I can get the jump on these people. They can't bust me if I bust myself first. Right? Here goes . . .

1. I sniff-check my socks.
2. I wet the bed until I was ten.
3. I'm proud to be an Okie from Muskogee.
4. I got so drunk in high school at my first coed dance that I threw up in the bathroom at St. Augustine's Academy.
5. I *still* enjoy hitchhiking in hot pants.
6. I sing "Mandy" when alone in my car.
7. The head of Alfredo Garcia is in a bowling-ball bag in my front-hall closet.
8. I got so drunk at Papa Joe's Bar on High Street at Ohio State University that four total strangers had to carry me back to my dorm.
9. I mix my plaids.
10. I wash and rinse but never "repeat."
11. I got so drunk last night I had sex with my husband.

12. I add MSG to everything.
13. I had Willie Nelson's face tattooed onto the left buttock of all my kids. No reason.
14. Once, as a room-service waitress in a fancy New York hotel, I stole the keys to Ray Charles's tour bus and drove my entire acting class to Fort Lauderdale for an impromptu spring break.
15. After my first C-section, I went an entire week without showering.
16. I throw away my kids' art projects almost immediately.
17. That last California earthquake was my fault. No pun intended.
18. I have a book from the church library that's two weeks overdue.
19. My favorite television show is now and always has been *Cops*.
20. I pick the longest line at the grocery store so I'll have time to read those tabloids cover to cover.

There's plenty of other stuff I did, and when you find out what those things are, let me know. 'Cause I want to make sure you heard it here first.

HAIL, CESAREAN:
THE KINDEST CUT

FROM THE MINUTE I found out I was pregnant, I knew everything was going to be perfect.

I've actually had this attitude about the world all my life. Every job I've ever auditioned for, I was sure I was going to get. It didn't really matter how many times I was rejected. I had a sort of blind faith, a blind drive (maybe I was just plain blind), which kept me going. Not that those rejections didn't hurt. But after a few hours, days, maybe a week, I would be right back at it.

So why should having a baby be any different? As far as I knew, my mother had vaginal deliveries, so there was nothing hereditary to suggest anything different for me. I had never been in the hospital for anything other than one or two mild asthma attacks, and once I became pregnant, that asthma went away, never to appear again.

See? Smooth sailing all the way.

So I knew I was in for a good time. Right before I discovered I was with child, I had been dieting for a movie part. (Talk about confidence—I was preparing for a role I hadn't even gotten yet!) As soon as the drugstore dipstick told me I was positive, Lord Loinly and I headed straight for Johnny Rocket's, where I proceeded to order everything on the menu and request other things that weren't ("Could you put some mayo in that chocolate malt?").

I had never been happier. Which was a little odd, because before I got married, the thought of children had never entered my mind. I was a reluctant baby-sitter, and found little kids boring.

But toward the end of our first year of marriage, I started getting the bug. One morning we woke up, and I said to Lord Wimbledon St. Bumbershoot, "Wouldn't it be great to hear two little feet pattering down the hallway, and see a little chubberwub appear at the door and climb into our bed?" A few months later I was pregnant.

Not only had we gotten pregnant easily, I could now drop the interminable dieting that plagues every actress on the planet. It was now my job to eat, and eat a lot—at least that was my interpretation of the situation.

I would prepare meals to tide me over while I was preparing my real meal, e.g., eat a toasted peanut butter and jelly sandwich to keep me going while I fried my eggs for breakfast. And no one could say a word! Who's going to chide a pregnant woman for gaining weight?

Other than my ob-gyn, I mean. There's some medical chart out there that states that a woman is only supposed to gain twenty to twenty-five pounds during pregnancy.

C'mon! What *man* came up with that statistic? The baby alone can weigh up to twelve pounds. Then there's the extra fifteen pounds on your breasts (fifteen *each*), the eighteen or so for your heinie, the ten on each hip, the five on each thigh, and then a few more ounces for all ten fingers and toes.

And it's all glorious fat. Healthy, glowing, fabulous corpulence. Except if you're on a TV show and your character is not with child. Which happened to me three out of the four times I was pregnant. Then it can be horrifying. But the first time it's magic. And since I have never experienced any morning sickness, there was no stopping me.

It was eat, eat, eat, morning, noon, and night. Joyous eating. Eating with abandon. Eating with complete strangers. I could not get enough. At restaurants, I would order soup, two appetizers, main course, dessert, and then whistle for the cheese cart. Think of the song from *Oliver!* "Food, Glorious Food," or whatever the hell it's called. It was *my* anthem.

Now, this is not to say that I didn't take care of myself. I did. I went to the gym regularly, working out every day. I wore tight-fitting leotards to show off my grand belly, and got compliments from guys who had never before looked at me twice. This was all possible with the first baby because I had no one else to run after. The only exercise I got during the other pregnancies was to lift a fork to my mouth and push a baby carriage around.

I think part of the reason I threw myself into the eating was to avoid thinking about the inevitable pain that was to come. I consider myself a somewhat tough person, but there is one pain that I find intolerable—abdominal cramping.

My *monthlies* were pretty terrifying, causing me to faint in the most public of places—restaurants, department stores, on my first day at a law firm where I was temping. (More on that later.) Once, many years before, someone had offhandedly remarked that labor was just like having your period, only a lot worse. I knew there was trauma ahead.

So even though Sir Manly St. Fertile and I took the Lamaze course (I think you get hauled into court by social services if you don't), I had no intention of trying to breathe my way through a seven- or eight-pounder splitting me in half.

Now, since I had a bit of a history of medicating myself to mask emotional pain, I certainly wasn't going to turn down a perfectly legal chemical cocktail to help me with real physical suffering.

The Lamaze course was a good way to become informed about all the razzamatazz that was going on inside. In fact, I was actually going to be too dozy to notice it at the time.

We took the express version of Lamaze and got it over with in one night. We told the instructor she could kind of skim over a lot, because I was determined to have an epidural. She nodded knowingly—as did every nurse on the ward when I was in labor.

Apparently people whose job it is to deliver babies have seen enough to know that there's better living through chemistry. And though I think a woman should be able to deliver her baby any way she wants to, I don't quite understand the pressure to "go natural."

I mean, I think if animals had the opportunity to have epidurals they would jump at the chance. In fact, what's "natural" is to try to avoid pain. Let's face it—I'm a wimp. I wanted plenty of doctors and nurses around me, and drugs in me.

As I got closer to my due date, I was able to eat less and less. Well, at one sitting, anyway. I had to break it up into about thirty-two small meals a day. And needless to say, I was suffering in the sartorial department.

Ten years ago, the maternity fashions didn't have quite the pizzazz that they do today, and I didn't have quite the money that I have today. But I needed something to tent myself in, so I headed out to the local maternity store.

Five hundred dollars later I left with a bad purple-and-white-striped top, purple leggings, and a flowered dress with a Peter Pan collar trimmed in lace. I hadn't worn a Peter Pan collar since the second grade, and lace has never been my thing. But apparently in those days, when you were impregnated, you suddenly turned into a delicate Victorian lady who had to wear floral patterns and take up embroidering. Designers have wised up in the last ten years, and now everybody lets it all hang out, covering up only when the labels say Gucci or Prada. Now every pregnant woman looks like an exotic belly dancer. I just looked like a belly. With a head and legs.

The joy of the whole thing starts wearing off about the seventh month. Especially when you've made it your mission to gain sixty pounds. Many of those pounds landed on my ankles and feet. The heat of July made it all worse. Everything started to swell, and even my nose looked big. I was ready to blow.

The baby was not. Two weeks past the due date, there was no sign of anything. My in-laws had flown in from England a week before I was supposed to pop, and had been sitting around our house putting together the umpteenth jigsaw puzzle to pass the time. We went on every sight-seeing tour, ate at every restaurant, rented every movie. Still no kid. Not even a fraction of dilation.

Finally, even my doctor had had it. I went in for my checkup, after which I had planned to go eat a nice big lunch and shop for some nice big shoes for my sausage feet. She took one last ultrasound, noticed the amniotic fluid was low, and said, "Okay, why don't you go over to the hospital and get hooked up." "Now?" I was stunned and completely unprepared (read: I hadn't showered). She was not kidding. A half hour later I was in my hospital gown with a Pitocin drip in my arm.

Since I had played an ob-gyn on *thirtysomething,* I knew what Pitocin was. I decided that, just out of curiosity, I would let the Pitocin work its magic for a while before I opted for any painkillers. After about two hours of walking up and down the hospital corridor, the cramping made me flash back to that first day on a temp job for a law firm. I had similar cramping then, and almost passed out in the bathroom. I spent the day lying on the desk in the office of a lawyer who was on vacation. I decided that one of those days was enough, and that if somebody was on hand who could rectify the situation, I would take her up on it.

Ah, the blessed epidural. Awesome. Do you remember, as a child, the horrible feeling of being nauseous, and then the sweet, sweet relief, the bliss, after you threw up? Multiply that bliss by a hundred, and you'll know what an epidural feels like.

I suddenly felt at one with the universe, and spent the next few hours thinking up ways to achieve world peace. Those wonderful anesthesiologists just kept feeding miracle chemicals into my blood, and it was brilliant.

Twenty hours later, after solving the world's problems, I was getting a bit testy and ready to give birth. However, my son was not ready to be born. I had hardly dilated, and was now running a temperature. I had vomited, lost control of everything below the waist, and swelled up like a blowfish. At one point, the pain guy said, "I have to run over to do a cesarean—I think there's enough morphine in there until I get back." I knew I was doomed.

Sure enough, the drugs started to wear off, and Dr. Feelgood was nowhere in sight. The contractions were coming pretty regularly, and, in the famous words of Glenn Close, I was not going to be ignored.

Every time a contraction came, I moaned with the best theatrical intensity I could muster. I had learned in acting school that my voice had to reach the last row in the theater, and this day I was making sure it was reaching the last anesthesiologist in L.A. Linda Blair had nothing on me. Lord Now What Have I Done was sweating bullets, feeling guilty as hell and helpless to boot.

Dr. Feelgood finally arrived, and as the drugs emptied into my bloodstream, I stopped howling mid-moan, turned to my husband with a glazed look in my eye, and said in a small, quiet voice, "Oh. That's better." He slowly backed away from my bed and out of the room.

It was no good. That baby wasn't dropping and I wasn't dilating. Everything was going a bit haywire, so the decision was made to cut me open. I felt bad. I had failed. I had blown another audition. Hubby had gotten over my multiple-personality disorder and was now beside me again, assuring me that everything was all right.

I was prepped for surgery. I guess that's what you call it. I was laid out on a table, my arms outstretched on either side of me and strapped down. A sheet was erected to shield me from the horror below my waist. And then something happened that no one had told me about, that had never been mentioned in any of the sixty-eight books I had read on the subject.

I started to shake.

I mean really shake. Especially my jaw. It felt like someone had inserted a set of those plastic wind-up choppers in my mouth and it was dancing around uncontrollably. The twenty-three hours of nonstop drugs had taken their toll, and I was like a junkie coming down off a three-day binge.

It only took about twenty minutes to get Sam out—the longest twenty minutes of my life. I heard a "Here he comes!" and then a lot of oohing and aahing. Everyone ran to the opposite end of the room, including Lord Manley St. Procreator, and proceeded to fawn over the new prince.

Meanwhile, I, the queen here, was left completely alone, strapped down, shaking and shivering, listening to the party at the other end of the room. The sheet was still blocking my view of everything, and all I could see as I turned my head was a little crucifix hanging on the wall. There He was, strapped down just like me, and all alone.

"At least *You* know I'm here," I thought.

After they put all my innards back and stitched me up,

Prince Sam was laid on my chest for the obligatory bonding nanosecond, and then he and I were whisked away in two different directions. The recovery room was full, so I found myself lying in the hallway, my teeth still chattering unmercifully.

My friend Felix had been hanging around in the waiting room and came by to see how I was doing. I was exhausted, shaking, alone, and dry as a bone. I hadn't had anything to eat or drink for a day and a half, and the doctors had given strict orders not to put anything in my stomach for a few more hours. "Screw that," Felix said, and that dear Samaritan brought me a cup of ice chips.

It took me about a day before I felt a connection with my new baby. I was shattered, sore, and still drugged up. It didn't help that little Sam just stared at me. He seemed a bit pissed off about the whole thing, and I was getting the blame. He finally gave in when he located my nipple, and we've been best friends ever since.

Hard to believe I opted to do it again three more times. Those little love bundles are pretty addictive, and I discovered that when you *plan* a C-section ahead of time, it's a whole different ball game.

The next delivery found me coiffed, manicured, pearls around my neck, and in and out of surgery in forty-five minutes. I then spent the next three days receiving friends, accepting gifts, watching talk shows, and basically being worshiped and adored. All the while blissed out on painkillers. Nice work if you can get it.

I could use about two more kids. I'm not really over it yet, and every time I see a baby my milk comes in. But I'm having a hard enough time getting the four I've got bathed, brushed, tucked in, read to, and kissed before ten P.M.

So I guess that's it for me. Although I've been thinking about adoption. Can you get a morphine drip when you do that?

CELEBRITY: PERK OR PROBLEM?
YOU MAKE THE CALL

TEN GOOD THINGS ABOUT BEING A CELEBRITY

1. Now that you're finally rich, you get everything free.
2. People *expect* you to cut in at the front of the line.
3. You've heard the expression "They think their s--t doesn't stink"? It's true. In fact, mine is peach ice cream.
4. Almost overnight, you get way smarter and your opinions on ecology and world affairs become really astute.
5. Your most insignificant daily activity takes on huge import. For example, someone will tell a tabloid, "I saw [name of celebrity] at the drugstore buying *postage stamps*! Can you believe it?"
6. You can now afford to send an assistant to the drugstore to buy your postage stamps.
7. You can schedule your face-lift between your manicure and your pedicure, and instead of being considered superficial, your friends will wonder why you didn't schedule that butt-lift as long as you were at it.

8. You can attend a charity event, one for which a free limousine is sent for you, free gourmet food is served to you, free first-class entertainment is played for you, and, at the end of the evening, a huge gift basket full of free TVs, DVDs, spa certificates, and jewelry is given to you. And for all this, you will be considered a great humanitarian.

9. Industry people who wouldn't have let you mow their lawn last year suddenly want you to play croquet on it next week. And they'll let you beat them.

10. You *might* get an obit in *The New York Times*.

TEN BAD THINGS ABOUT BEING A CELEBRITY

1. Sometimes crazy people think they're you.

2. People assume you have way more money than you really do.

3. Once pictures of you begin appearing everywhere all the time, the whole world begins consciously documenting how tragically you've aged on a daily basis. And they're right.

4. You are fair game for being interrupted at any time and any place by everyone you ever met and thousands more you don't even know.

5. If you don't settle old scores with siblings—to their advantage—they will sell embarrassing overweight childhood photos of you to the *Weekly World News*, where you will be cut-and-pasted next to aliens from outer space. Or Bill Clinton.

6. Everybody knows your name. But that idiot actor presenting to you at an awards show will *still* mispronounce it.

7. If you gain ten pounds, the press will say you have an out-of-control eating disorder. If you lose ten pounds, the press will say you have an out-of-control eating disorder. The only way to keep the press from commenting about your weight is to be pregnant, all the time.

8. There's always someone *more* famous than you, and they always show up right before you at that event where you were hoping to get a lot of press coverage.

9. People keep saying they loved you on *Three's Company*.

10. It all ends at some point, but you still have to make a living. And because you were once famous, the only jobs now available to you are embarrassing infomercials (if they'll have you), embarrassing game shows (if they'll have you), and embarrassing reunion specials of your sitcom (if they can find your phone number).

GOLDEN SHOES
FOR MOM

I WAS ONCE BOOKED on a cable talk show that was part of a women's network. As I waited in the makeup room to go on, I watched the segment before mine, in which the anniversary of the Pill's legalization in America was being commemorated.

As part of the segment, two women doctors were discussing the significance of the Pill in our society. (Just a little note of interest—their names were Dr. Weiner and Dr. Seiman—I kid you not.) When asked how the Pill changed life for American women, Dr. Weiner said, "The Pill freed women so they could do more than just have babies." The interviewer nodded sagely in agreement.

That comment really pissed me off. And not just the comment. The blithe acceptance of it was equally distressing. A few minutes later I was called to do my interview, and before we got into it, I mentioned that Dr. Weiner had really exposed her true colors, disrespecting moms and homemakers by writing them off. The host of my segment thought I was overreacting.

That host was single and childless and young, and the sentiment behind that comment has been so woven into her subconscious that she never even noticed it.

And that sentiment is everywhere. Hillary Clinton made the big mistake of expressing it during her husband's first run for the presidency when she defended her work as a lawyer by saying "What should I have done? Stayed home and baked cookies?" She tried to blow it off as a joke, but I thought it was truly revealing.

As an actor, I spent years training to look not at the words in a script but at what was behind them. And after years in therapy, I learned that there are no jokes. So I don't buy that Hillary was just kidding. And the scrambling around to look domestic immediately afterward confirmed something for me: she has a certain disdain for women who are full-time homemakers, because she's under the mistaken impression that the entire experience of being a full-time mom revolves around cooking and cleaning.

All right, I'll admit it, there *is* a lot of cooking and cleaning involved. In fact, when I'm on my summer hiatus, I find that I rarely leave the kitchen and the attached laundry room. But there are a million other things that are accomplished in those rooms that go way beyond domestic labor.

Someone once told me that baking is a science, cooking an art. It's true. The amount of chemistry, physics, math, and imagination that my boys have learned just by hanging out in the kitchen is not calculable.

When Danny poured his OJ into his milk, we all learned about coagulation. When Joe burned his hand on the stove, we learned about temperature and metal as a conductor. When Sam nuked his crayons, we learned about microwaves and how much it costs to replace one. When John flushed my lace tablecloth down the toilet, we learned about mom's blood pressure and what happens when it goes through the roof.

There is spiritual growth that takes place every time they say grace before a meal. And I try to make somewhat socially acceptable beings out of them by disallowing farting noises at the table, or any conversation that includes the words *poop* or *peepee*.

Even their dexterity is improved as they learn how to use a fork, even if it's for flipping food at their brothers. And Joe has learned to climb up the drawers like a mountain goat to get at the cups for a drink of water.

They've learned matching and sorting when I make them help with the laundry or unload the dishwasher. They also learn a sense of accomplishment.

It's not so important that a mom is good at any of this stuff. What is important is that she's there to give it a shot.

It's little stuff, and it takes place almost imperceptibly throughout the day. But it's what sticks with a kid. My mom showed me how to make meat loaf and Toll House cookies. She was always there, and I never realized how much that meant until she was gone.

Right about now, you might be thinking that this is all a bit hypocritical, coming from a mom who works. But the reason I can say all of this is because I'm acutely aware of what I'm missing when I'm at the studio. I've been fortunate in that

I am able to bring my kids to work, but by the time I'm nearing my summer hiatus, I can tell they've had enough of my television-mom lifestyle. And I have too. I want to be a real mom. I can't wait to cook them a meal, take them to the dentist, volunteer at school.

And speaking of school, those institutions would cease to exist if there weren't stay-at-home moms to pick up the slack. I am ever so grateful to all those women who do the thankless jobs of organizing the fund-raisers, book drives, Scout meetings, and piano recitals. They shuttle vans of kids around, arrange play dates, bring snacks to the soccer games. They make costumes, write newsletters, and generally make life easier for people like me and fun for the kids.

These moms do such an invaluable service for the whole community, but it's the type of thing that you can't give a dollar value to. Which seems to be the only way society knows how to judge the worthwhile-ness of something. The benefits don't really show up until years later, after the kids survive their twenties, come back to their senses, and become productive human beings.

This is not to say that women shouldn't work outside the home. But they also should not be considered invisible when they opt for full-time motherhood. I've experienced this myself at times.

When I was pregnant with my first, I was at a party with a large group of industry people. I wasn't working at the time, and I ended up sitting by myself watching clusters of guests ignore me while discussing the various projects they were involved in. People literally could not think of anything to say to me once they found out that my whole raison d'être was to gestate.

One person took pity on me. Alfred Molina, a terrific English actor, happened to get the last seat, which happened to be next to me. What a jolly soul! He couldn't have cared less whether I was working, and because we didn't have that to talk about, we got into deeper, more personal things. He chatted with me for an hour, and I have never been more grateful. He remains a dear friend to this day.

Now, it's good for children to learn independence, and to see their mom accomplish things in her own right, but there is something primal and irreplaceable about Mom around the house. And you don't even have to be that good at it. You don't have to be great at basketball or make pancakes shaped like teddy bears. (Early on I bought a kids' cookbook in which the author had made every meal to look like *something*—stars, animals, flowers. She should be *shot*.)

My kids mostly just want to watch a movie together, to lean against me with a blanket around all of us and cuddle in front of the umpteenth viewing of *Star Wars*. They want to hear stories from when I was their age, and about how I fought with their aunts and uncle. They want to help me sort out closets and to check their homework.

Of course, things are a sight better today than they were in the fifties; stay-at-home moms have the advantages of health clubs, book clubs, higher education, and Oprah for everything else. There are more opportunities for women to educate and expand their minds, all of which benefit their children.

Which is really what it's all about: giving the next generation the tools to experience and improve the world around them in order to make this a better place. Because as much as we'd like to believe otherwise, we're all going to be forgotten somewhere down the line. We'll certainly be forgotten by the world, and eventually by our own families. I mean, who can name their great-great-great-grandmother? And if you can, do you really know anything about her?

So it's really all about what we give to our children. And hopefully we'll realize a dream or two of our own along the way.

I recently found a book that brought all this home to me. Written in 1939 by Du Bose Heyward, *The Country Bunny and the Little Gold Shoes* is a gift that every mom should give herself. It tells the tale of a little country-girl bunny who dreams of growing up and being the Easter bunny. She is laughed at by all the long-legged jackrabbits and the fine white bunnies in big houses. She ends up getting married and having twenty-one (!) baby bunnies. She forgets about her plans to be an Easter bunny, and instead devotes herself to training her children. She teaches them to sweep, make beds, cook, wash up, sew, sing, paint, and garden. And the last little one she makes keeper of her chair, to pull it out whenever she comes to dinner.

One day years later, the little country bunny hears that a new Easter bunny is going to be selected. She gathers up her children and goes to watch the fun, thinking that she is just an old mother bunny who would never be picked. When the kind old grandfather bunny sees her there with her children, he realizes that she must have all the skills to be an Easter bunny: goodness, kindness, wisdom, swiftness, and cleverness.

She becomes an Easter bunny, but on her last delivery to a

sick little boy, she becomes injured and unable to continue. The kind old grandfather bunny shows up, and instead of chiding her for failing in her duties, he commends her for her bravery, and gives her a pair of golden shoes, which helps her to finish her delivery.

I almost wept when I finished this story. (My two little ones couldn't figure out what was wrong with me.) Being a good mother takes a lot of skill, patience, and talent. It incorporates so many gifts in the service of others. The benefits of years of mothering are often not noticed until long after that mother is gone. And yet it probably benefits the world more than any corporation ever could.

George Eliot sums it up at the end of her novel *Middlemarch* when she writes of the character Dorothea:

> Her full nature, like that river of which Cyrus broke the strength, spent itself in channels which had no great name on the earth. But the effect of her being on those around her was incalculably diffusive: for the growing good of the world is partly dependent on unhistoric acts; and that things are not so ill with you and me as they might have been, is half doing to the number who lived faithfully a hidden life, and rest in unvisited tombs.

God bless all moms out there; the stay-at-homes, the working moms, and especially the single moms. Whenever you get tired, discouraged, or feel unappreciated, go to God for that pair of golden shoes, and know that all your efforts are affecting not just the lives of your children but the direction of the world.

HUSBANDS:
AN OWNER'S MANUAL

A PROFESSOR at Duke University Divinity School, Stanley Hauerwas, taught something he called Hauerwas's Law: You always marry the wrong person.

Thank you, Professor Hauerwas, for confirming what I've known from the beginning.

I believe that, for women, there is no avoiding marrying the wrong person, because we often marry men. And men are just plain wrong.

We don't seem to notice this when we are young. In pre- and elementary school, we don't really notice boys at all, except when they are gross and we scream "Cooties!" and run.

Later they become of interest, if only to have something to laugh about with our girlfriends.

But at some point we lose all reason and find them irresistibly attractive, and spend inordinate amounts of money on perfecting ourselves for them and way too much time thinking about them, talking about them, scheming to nab them.

And for the few months or years of courtship, we do crazy things together like going clothes shopping and attending sporting events.

Then they blow a bunch of hard-earned cash for a ring and subject themselves to the torture that is wedding planning.

Pretty shortly after that, we realize it was all a huge mistake.

All my friends seemed to have realized this around the same time, usually after giving birth to their second or third child. And all our husbands seem to be guilty of all the same crimes: not helping, being insensitive, putting sports (both watching them and playing them) above all else, and bugging us for sex too often (more than once a month) and at the most inconvenient times (which would be just about any hour of the day or night, especially bedtime—the last thing a gal wants to do after a long, hard day).

So, what's the secret to a happy marriage? I've read a lot of books on the topic (or at least skimmed through them or glanced at chapter headings), and I've gleaned a thing or two that occasionally works.

Here are a few things you ought to know in order to get your husband running smoothly and efficiently. I want to make a point here that none of these remarks, comments, criticisms, or suggestions reflect in any way on *my* husband, Lord Bagsby Frothingwell St. Dingdong-on-the-Thames, who is perfect in every way. I don't take any credit. I just got lucky, that's all.

First thing you do is tell your husband he is perfect in every way. Here's why this works so well. All men feel deep down inside that they are, in fact, *perfect in every way*. It's their mothers' fault. If you happen to mention that you also find this true, they will think you're a genius and will be much more likely to do almost any dang thing you tell them.

Here's another little secret. Most husbands will do anything for that *other* thing. Now, I know that sex is a sacred bond of marriage intended for the glory of God and the deepening of the union between two bodies and souls, not some physical rigmarole offered in exchange for a Gucci bag that was on sale anyway, for Pete's sake! Not that I have any experience in this area.

But think about it. Really, what's three minutes out of your week? (I'm counting that as sex twice, Wednesday and Saturday.) What's three minutes compared to having Mr. Moody Uncooperative Whiner and Nitpicker of the Checkbook (the bag was on sale!) skulking around the house like a wounded animal for a week. Or longer.

(My husband always lets me know when he's not getting enough. The other night when my boys were being particularly rambunctious, I yelled at them, "In this house, we don't touch each other's privates!" To which my husband replied, "No kidding.")

You know what else is really effective in getting the wild man domesticated? Tone. In fact, tone is everything. In the course of a marriage you will say the same thing to your husband many, many times. (Don't even get me started on the kids. The number of times you repeat things to *them*—"Leave your brother *alone!*"—is beyond the calculating capabilities of most mainframe computers.)

But there is the opportunity while communicating with a

husband to manage the emotional volume of the exchange through your tone. A simple request such as "Could you take out the garbage?" can take on myriad forms of meaning depending on the tone.

Could you take out the garbage? The implication is that the man is incapable. Which in turn implies some lack of physical prowess on his part. Don't do that.

Could *you* take out the garbage? Here it sounds as if the wife always does this loathsome, lowly task which was designed by the laws of God and nature to be performed by the male of the species and any deviation from that plan is an abomination. And that's exactly right.

Could you *take* out the garbage? It's easy to see that the emphasis on the word *take* implies that the husband in question only *contributes* to the growth of garbage without ever *removing* it.

Could you take *out* the garbage? Same as above.

Could you take out *the* garbage? This can be paraphrased as can you *at least* take out the garbage? As if it might be the only thing he does around the house all year. And only on one weekend, when my parents are visiting. When his parents visit, his *mom* takes out the garbage.

Could you take out the *garbage*? This is the worst, or most explicit, example of negative tone. When the emphasis is on the last word, it means the *real* last word of the sentence is missing but hugely present in its absence. The sentence really sounds like: Could you take out the garbage, *ass----*? And that kind of talk doesn't accomplish anything. Even if the plastic bags do end up out on the curb.

Keep it up and so will the marriage.

One of the books I read on husband and wife communication urged that, instead of fighting when they become angry at the way they are being talked to, couples should say the word *tone* when they feel they are being unfairly accosted verbally.

His Lordship, St. Arthur Treacher's Fish and Chips, and I tried that once without much success. It began with me nicely asking him to take out the garbage and him saying "Tone." So I *toned* his tone. He *toned* my toning of his tone. Our marriage counselor told us we were both tone-deaf, although I can carry a tune. My husband thought Tone Def would be a cool name for a rap group or a record label.

Another book we read proposed the theory that all the problems in marriage are about communication, and that if couples apply cognitive-thinking principles to their relationships, great avenues of understanding will open up and meaningful exchanges will take place.

This worked for a while. My husband would casually drop some outrageously loaded statement, like "What are we having for dinner?" My usual reply would have been "Stop HOUND-ING me!" or "GET OFF MY BACK!" or "So, when exactly were your arms AMPUTATED?" But after applying cognitive communication to the problem, the exchange sounded something more like this:

HIM: What are we having for dinner?
ME: You know, when you ask me that, it makes me feel as if you expect *me* to plan a meal every night.

HIM: I do.

ME: Well, I feel myself getting angry at your assumption that because I'm a woman, I will automatically do the cooking.

HIM: And the cleaning.

ME: Exactly.

HIM: And your problem is . . . ?

The cognitive thing got too confusing. And I think I threw something at him.

The addition of children can sometimes improve the situation. You're both too tired or too busy to argue, have sex, golf (him), or shop (you). That eliminates a lot of the hot buttons. Of course, many new buttons are added: feeding the kids, bathing the kids, reading to the kids, playing with the kids, putting the kids to bed. The difference is, if you have any desire to have your children grow up to be marginally healthy mentally, you won't have screaming matches in front of them. Instead, the arguments, accusations, and blaming will all be expressed in whispered hisses through clenched teeth, or not at all, replaced with a week of silent seething and then a shopping binge followed by lunch with your girlfriend, where you'll drink three margaritas and sound off about this big mistake you've made.

Then you'll come home and he'll have done something really annoying, like bought flowers for you or helped the kids with their homework, or he'll let you watch the figure skating (maybe even watch it *with* you), and you'll feel terribly guilty and ashamed and you'll call your friend and apologize for saying all those things because he's not really that bad and you must be just about to get your period.

Then there's one more sneaky thing they do to get you on their side. No, it's not when they buy you jewelry because you went through thirty-two hours of labor, or how they are able to set up the VCR, the DVD, the receiver, and the satellite box plus program the figure skating so it will record automatically for you; no, not all that.

It's when they make sure the kids look a little or a lot like them, and have some of their traits. So that when you fall in love with your little guy, you start seeing your husband in him, and you think about what your husband must have been like as a little boy. And you see Junior do something just the way your husband does it, and you remember that you used to think it was cute when your husband did it too, and maybe it still is kind of cute, and maybe your husband isn't so bad after all.

Sometimes it even makes you want to have another baby.

Men are such jerks.

A FINAL WORD
ON FAMILY

RECENTLY MY HUSBAND AND I decided that from four o'clock on, the TV, the cell phones, the Game Boys, and the Internet had to go off. We came to this decision after one of our huge yearly fights about . . . well, I can't remember what it was about, but it was big, and now we don't have the electronic distraction anymore. As a result, we actually talk to each other at night instead of zoning out after slogging our way through dinner, homework, and baths with the kids. Which is the other thing. It's not such a slog with the kids since the boob tube isn't providing a constant stream of nerve-jangling noise in the background. In other words, peace.

Which is something we could all use more of these days. And not just world peace. Peace in our homes. Fewer activities, less scheduling, more time for hanging out, daydreaming, and puttering. Because at the end of the day, all we can be sure about is that we love one another and that we've tried our best that day to show it. All the other stuff, all our best-laid plans, have no guarantees, as we were all reminded on September 11.

I had a lot of best-laid plans that week. In fact, the entire cast of *Raymond* headed to the Big Apple on September 10 after months of preparing for the premiere of our sixth season and our launch into syndication. So not only had the cast been booked onto numerous talk shows and radio and print interviews, but all the writers and their spouses were being treated to the trip courtesy of our executive producer, Phil Rosenthal, who was also taking everyone to a celebratory dinner at the famous Peter Luger Steak House in Brooklyn. On top of that, my husband, Dave, was joining me for a few days for a much-needed "parents only" trip. We had finally gotten tickets to *The Producers* and were all set up to see friends and do a little business for our production company on the side.

It was cold and rainy when we finally reached our hotel that night, but we couldn't have woken up to a more glorious morning—I could tell it was going to be a fantastic trip! While Dave slept, I arose at six-thirty and went to the next suite to have my hair and makeup done. An hour later, I was in the hotel lobby to meet the rest of the cast for our first talk-show appearance of the day when I heard the doorman say that a plane had crashed into the World Trade Center. It seemed like a really tragic accident, until another doorman announced that it had happened again, and then we all knew it was intentional. Not yet grasping the enormity of it all, we headed into the limo and wondered how we were going to do a talk show in the midst of this. The problem was solved when we arrived at Rockefeller Plaza and were told that the building was being evacuated and our interview had been canceled.

We headed back to the hotel, and then we all went to our rooms and called our families. Notice what happens when The End of the World looms large? What's the first thing *everyone* does? Call family. Well, first I had to wake Dave, who kept shouting from his bed that he didn't need housekeeping as I pounded on the door. When he finally woke all the way up and let me in, he couldn't believe what I was telling him; I couldn't believe it myself. We turned on the TV just in time to hear that the Pentagon had been hit, then, minutes later, the towers collapsed.

Not knowing what else the day would bring, I called our nanny, Malin, and told her to keep the kids inside. As we picked up more information from the television, the horror washed over us in waves. The need to be with our families propelled us down to Phil's room. If we couldn't be with our real family, our TV family would do in a pinch.

There was nothing to do but sit and watch the TV together. Being together was a true blessing; it was comforting to have these dear friends all in one room, discussing the events, trading the rumors that kept flying about, and plotting how we would get home. And we ate. The breakfast buffet from our morning interviews was transferred up to Phil's room, and you've never seen a hungrier bunch of people. I myself was ravenous. Although I didn't feel scared or nervous—it was all too over-the-top to feel real—I couldn't stop eating. Or sleeping. So that must be how I react to stress. After an hour of watching the horrifying footage and feeling helpless to do anything about anything, I excused myself for a nap.

That feeling of helplessness frustrated everyone. It was hard to sit in that hotel, knowing that a few blocks away people's worlds were falling apart. My hairdresser, Brett, decided to go find someplace to donate blood. Ray and his manager, Rory Rosegarten, went for a walk in Central Park to take a breather from the endless outpouring of bad news. While there in the park they came upon a man covered from head to toe in ashes. He looked as if he had been in the Mount Saint Helen's volcano eruption. In fact, the man had walked out of lower Manhattan and was lucky to be alive. "Keith the Insurance Guy," as he came to be known, had been caught in the fallout, and had just started walking uptown, not sure of where he was going or what he was supposed to do. His wife and new baby girl were in New Jersey, and he was stuck in the New York City lockdown. No one was coming in, nobody was getting out. Not on September 11.

Ray and Rory took Keith back to the Essex House, where Rory gave him his hotel room and Ray gave him some clean, if dorky, clothes to wear. (We all noticed that Keith's butt looked a lot better in Ray's jeans than Ray's did.) Keith called his family and told them that he was all right and that he would get home as soon as he was able to. Dave and I caught up with them later on as they strolled the Upper West Side. And then we all spent the day and night together.

Keith the Insurance Guy became like a new member of the

cast of *Everybody Loves Raymond.* He told us what he had seen and heard and felt that morning and how he was feeling increasingly fortunate to be still walking around on the planet. That night we all went out to dinner with our new friend Keith and had a quiet, kind of warm evening together. As happens in the midst of fear and uncertainty, there was a lot of joking around, and the food never tasted better. In the same way that we on the show had become closer and more familial through the disaster, it had also enabled us to bring Keith into the fold for some rest and comfort throughout the relatively short time he was separated from his loved ones.

The next day Ray was able to get Keith a car to drive him home to his family. He was anxious to see them, and even though we had spent only a day and night with him, we all felt bonded. After all, he had walked out of the eye of the hurricane into our lives for a little while. And he had allowed us to feel special by performing a small act of kindness for him. We had done a little something for one New Yorker, which was a whole lot better than nothing.

Before he left, Keith told us that his family knew where he worked and would have no problem believing he had walked out of the seventh circle of hell virtually unscathed. But he said they would never believe, not in a million years, that he had spent the day and the night with his new best friends, the cast of *Everybody Loves Raymond.*

The rest of us had to hang for a bit longer, until the airspace opened up again. That is, those of us who were flying home. Ray and Brad, being the most paranoid of the bunch, decided the safest thing to do was to be driven home cross-country on a bus. (They made it as far as Tennessee, bailed out, and rented a van until Little Rock, where they finally conceded to taking a charter the rest of the way.) I forced my husband to take a separate charter, because with all that was going on, I didn't want to take the chance of leaving my kids orphans. I felt anxious getting into that little plane, and we were all grateful when we touched down—the California night had never seemed more beautiful.

And neither had my kids. I hugged them that night, thinking about all the kids whose mom or dad wouldn't be coming home. Having experienced the death of my own mother when I was twelve, I know the pain many of those families will be going through for the next few months, the next few years.

Those families will survive this, and go on with their lives. We'll all survive this, and we'll never be the same. But the changes we experience can make us better people, better friends, better spouses, better parents. The things we thought were important, all our priorities, completely shifted in the space of a day. I try not to be so impatient with the boys (including Dave) anymore. My "to do" list has become shorter, and if that doesn't get done, I don't sweat it. And I've taken to heart the saying on a plaque that my stepmom, Cece, gave me, a saying that I had always thought to be a bit corny: "Live Well, Laugh Often, Love Much." I get it now.

So, if you have been good enough not only to have bought this book but even to have read it to the very last page, I have one piece of advice for you: Close this book, get up out of your chair, and go hug your nearest family member. Life is so precious.

One more piece of advice: You might want to brush your teeth before hugging anyone.

You probably have book-breath.

> *Thanks,*
> *Patricia Heaton*

ABOUT THE AUTHOR

PATRICIA HEATON graduated from Ohio State University and made her Broadway debut in the gospel musical *Don't Get God Started*. She has appeared in numerous television films and series, and in feature films including *Memoirs of an Invisible Man*, *Beethoven*, *The New Age*, and *Space Jam*. For her role in *Everybody Loves Raymond*, she won the Emmy for Leading Actress in a Comedy Series in 2000 and again in 2001. She lives with her husband and four sons in Los Angeles.